General editor: Graham Handley

Brodie's Notes on E.M. Forster's

Howards End

Ray Wilcox

macmillan

First published 1979 by Pan Books Ltd

This revised edition published 1993 by
THE MACMILLAN PRESS LTD
Houndmills, Basingstoke, Hampshire RG21 2XS
and London
Companies and representatives
throughout the world

ISBN-10 033358094X
ISBN-13 9780333580943
Printed and bound in Great Britain by
CPI Antony Rowe, Chippenham and Eastbourne

Logging, pulping and manufacturing processes are
expected to conform to the environmental regulations
of the country of origin.

Contents

Preface

The intention throughout this study aid is to stimulate and guide, to encourage your involvement in the book, and to develop informed responses and a sure understanding of the main details.

Brodie's Notes provide a clear outline of the play or novel's plot, followed by act, scene, or chapter summaries and/or commentaries. These are designed to emphasize the most important literary and factual details. Poems, stories or non-fiction texts combine brief summary with critical commentary on individual aspects or common features of the genre being examined. Textual notes define what is difficult or obscure and emphasize literary qualities. Revision questions are set at appropriate points to test your ability to appreciate the prescribed book and to write accurately and relevantly about it.

In addition, each of these Notes includes a critical appreciation of the author's art. This covers such major elements as characterization, style, structure, setting and themes. Poems are examined technically – rhyme, rhythm, for instance. In fact, any important aspect of the prescribed work will be evaluated. The aim is to send you back to the text you are studying.

Each study aid concludes with a series of general questions which require a detailed knowledge of the book: some of these questions may invite comparison with other books, some will be suitable for coursework exercises, and some could be adapted to work you are doing on another book or books. Each study aid has been adapted to meet the needs of the current examination requirements. They provide a basic, individual and imaginative response to the work being studied, and it is hoped that they will stimulate you to acquire disciplined reading habits and critical fluency.

Graham Handley 1990

A close reading of the set book is the student's primary task. These Notes will help to increase your understanding and appreciation of the book, and to stimulate *your own* thinking about it: *they are in no way intended as a substitute* for a thorough knowledge of the book.

Page references in these Notes are to the Penguin edition of *Howards End*, but references are usually given to particular chapters, so that the Notes may be used with any edition of the novel.

The author and his work

Edward Morgan Forster was born in 1879 in London. His father, an architect, died before he was born and he was brought up by women, his mother and a great-aunt, Marianne Thornton, of whom he later wrote a memoir. It was his great-aunt who left him a legacy of eight thousand pounds, a considerable sum in those days when it is remembered that Margaret Schlegel in *Howards End* lives very well on six hundred a year. This inheritance enabled him to write in independence and security.

As a child he lived in Hertfordshire in the house on which Howards End is modelled. He went as a day-boy to Tonbridge School, where he was miserable. A disguised description of his days there can be found in *The Longest Journey*. Then he went to King's College, Cambridge, where he felt at home. He was much influenced by the teaching of the philosopher G. E. Moore, who believed that the most important things in life were the enjoyment of beauty and the cultivation of personal relations.

After Cambridge, Forster travelled with his mother to Italy. Both *Where Angels Fear to Tread* (1905) and *A Room with a View* (1900) are set there: both novels use the contrast between Italy and England; in both, Italian values show up English middle-class stupidity and hypocrisy. *The Longest Journey* (1907) is a larger work than these, a celebration of the freedom of friendship as opposed to the slavery of marriage.

Howards End was published in 1910. After reading the book, one is surprised to discover that its author was only thirty when he wrote it. During his lifetime he published only one more novel, *A Passage to Indian* (1924). He had visited India twice, and the novel records the life of the British Raj; it is an immensely subtle account of the relations between the Indians and the British, with an appeal for a 'connection' to be made between the values of the two societies. After Forster's death in 1970, another novel, *Maurice*, was published. It has a homosexual theme, and it seems unfinished, or at least unpolished. Before the First World War Forster also wrote many short stories. Most of these are fantastic or allegorical. They appear in *The Celestial Omnibus* (1911), and *The Eternal Moment* (1928).

In the second half of his life Forster was known chiefly as an essayist, critic and broadcaster. His essays appear in two collections, *Abinger Harvest* (1936) and *Two Cheers for Democracy* (1951). In 1927 he gave the Clark Lectures at Cambridge, which were published under the title of *Aspects of the Novel*. The last years of his life were spent in rooms at King's College, Cambridge.

Plot summary

Nobody, I imagine, would think that the plot of *Howards End* represents one of the book's main claims to fame. It is too dependent on coincidence and melodrama. Forster's genius does not include a talent for describing action and external event; and when he comes to critical and dramatic points in the machinery of his story he often finds ways of avoiding them. A favourite device is to describe them *after* they have happened, through the eyes of one of the participants. Thus he avoids describing the night Helen spends with Leonard – there would, in any event, have been trouble with the censor – but gives the story, many months later, through Helen's eyes. When he cannot avoid one of the more melodramatic points in his plot he is manifestly awkward and embarrassed. The scene in which Jacky confronts her ex-lover, Henry Wilcox, is almost ludicrously strained and unconvincing, and so is the scene in which Charles kills Leonard – where 'the long arm of coincidence' is surely made to reach too far.

Two quotations from Forster's *Aspects of the Novel* are worth considering (the whole book is essential reading). 'Yes – oh dear yes – the novel tells a story. That is the fundamental aspect without which it could not exist ... and I wish that it was not so, that it could be something different – melody, or perception of the truth, not this low atavistic form.' One must make allowance for a degree of tongue-in-cheek here, and it is true that Forster goes on to make a distinction between story and plot, but one feels that the drive to tell a story, in the simplest sense of the word, to keep even the most unsophisticated reader wondering what will happen next, is an important quality of the novelist in which Forster is somewhat lacking. He supplies a story, but reluctantly, or, to use his own word, 'sadly'. He is a continuously interesting writer, but for other reasons. Moreover, it seems at times that his story is sometimes at odds with what he is really trying to say. The epigraph of the story is 'Only connect', but the events of the story would seem to indicate the dangers of trying to do so.

In his chapter 'The Plot' in the same book, Forster had something more positive to say. He denies Aristotle's assertion that 'All human happiness and misery take the form of action' and goes on: 'we believe that happiness and misery exist in the secret life, which each of us leads privately and to which (in his characters) the novelist has access. And by the secret life we mean the life for which there is no external evidence ... a chance word or sigh are just as much evidence as a speech or a murder: the life they reveal ceases to be secret and enters the realm of action.'

This reminds us that the real crises in *Howards End* are not, in fact, the dramatic highlights of external event. The importance of Jacky's association with Henry lies not in itself but in Henry's reaction to its revelation, particularly the fact that it never crosses his mind that he has offended against Ruth. Both Henry and Margaret face crucial tests, but they occur in the course of conversation, not in the realm of action: Margaret is asked by Ruth Wilcox to come and stay at Howards End, Henry is asked by Margaret to allow Helen to stay at Howards End. Margaret passes her test eventually; Henry fails his.

The plot provides the framework, though not always a completely satisfactory framework, within which Forster can explore a number of themes. One of these is the condition of England and the growth of the 'civilization of luggage'. He sees the England which he loves breaking down, and he hates what he sees. The coming of the motor-car is only a way of creating dust and enabling one to pass through Westmorland without noticing it; the paddock at Howards End makes way for a garage. In fact, Forster uses the motor-car as a symbol of disorientating change. London becomes a property-developer's dream where the constant flux is good for trade. People are cut off from the past by the rate of change and from the earth by urban sprawl. Everything becomes increasingly as it is everywhere else, as difference and distinction are obliterated. London is 'creeping' and London is the enemy. 'One visualizes it as a tract of quivering gray, intelligent without purpose, and excitable without love; as a spirit that has altered before it can be chronicled; as a heart that certainly beats, but with no pulsation of humanity' (Chapter 13, p. 116). The kind of business organization that Henry Wilcox represents creates armies of wage-slaves like Leonard Bast – whose work is boring and dehumanizing, who have lost the life of the body and who are debarred from the life of the spirit. Sometimes Forster topples into sentimentality, as in some of the lyrical passages of description, and sometimes into an irritation mysticism – or merely mist: but, even before the First World War, he is diagnosing a real and frightening process. 'Month by month the roads smelt more strongly of petrol, and were more difficult to cross, and human beings heard each other speak with great difficulty, breathed less of the air, and saw less of the sky' (Chapter 13, p. 115).

Against this there is the 'hunt for a home', which Forster says is the theme of his novel. The title of the book is the name of a house, and houses play a large part in it. For Henry Wilcox a house is a disposable tissue – except that he hopes to dispose of it at a profit. The Wilcoxes, as Helen points out, own a large number of houses and are constantly improving and changing them. For Ruth Wilcox, on the other hand, a house is a place in which to put down roots; to convert into a home; a whole world to live and die in. The greatest calamity – it would kill her – is to be uprooted. But it takes a human being like Ruth to achieve this sort of identification with a home. Mr Wilcox's flat in Ducie Street has furniture which suggests that 'a motor-car had spawned'. The ideal home is a link between the past and the future, a guarantee of stability and the best flower of civilization.

The words 'only connect' are clearly the master-phrase of the novel. Connections are attempted between a wide diversity of things: materialism and idealism, masculine and feminine, the beast and the monk, prose and passion. The plot dramatizes the Schlegels' experiments in connection: creaks and all, it is designed to bring the three families of the Basts, the Schlegels and the Wilcoxes into relation with one another.

Helen reaches down through the social classes to make 'connection' with Leonard, who lives on the edge of the abyss. The Schlegel sisters live comfortably – too comfortably – on their islands of six hundred a year and feel a conscience about it, though their brother Tibby allows himself to be corrupted into sloth by his financial security. Leonard is trying to heave himself upwards by acquiring a veneer of culture. Helen's attempt to help him fails and, indirectly, she kills him. Helen is too hysterical and absolutist, is in herself too lacking in proportion to be able to help anyone; Henry is too indifferent to care, and perhaps the cards are stacked too strongly against Leonard for it to be possible for anyone to help him. Helen tries to play God without having the wisdom or the omnipotence of God, and she uses Leonard as a stick to beat the Wilcoxes with; she is herself overcome by the 'panic and emptiness' which she so loathes and fears in the Wilcoxes. It seems that Mr Wilcox's philosophy, except that it is based on smugness, is right: 'We live and let live and assume that things are jogging along fairly well elsewhere.'

Margaret attempts, through her marriage with Henry Wilcox, to connect the poetry and the prose, the business world and the intellectual, the private and the public. She wants to 'save' him, and at least she sets about the task with more tact, patience and understanding than Helen shows towards Leonard, because she is a wiser person; but her failure is as complete, as she should have forseen that it would be. She has taken on, in Henry, a particularly intransigent example of the male ego. He is too obtuse, morally dishonest and self-satisfied to be able to make any connections at all. After Margaret's great indictment of his double standards in Chapter 38, Forster adds, speaking through her consciousness:

'It was spoken not only to her husband but to thousands of men like him – a protest against the inner darkness in high places that comes with a commercial age ... He had refused to "connect", on the clearest issue that can be laid before a man, and their love must take the consequences' (Chapter 43, p. 322). In the end Henry is broken, and Margaret is left to 'make what she can of him', which seems to amount to not much more than putting a rug round his knees.

It is very possible to be impatient with the Schlegel sisters, to regard them as interfering busybodies who try, and conspicuously fail, to rebuild the world in their own image. The only important relationship that survives unshattered is their relationship with each other; and at the end of the book they dismiss with a remarkable lack of concern the damage they have done. Leonard has had an adventure, and that, they seem to say, is good enough for him. But surely Forster doesn't *intend* us to regard them as busybodies, equally smug – if with more reason – as Henry?

The end of the novel is curiously unsatisfactory as the two sisters settle down into their private world, knitting out their time in security and shared happiness, still sitting on their financially protected 'islands', and weeping no tears over the death and destruction of all those who have opposed them. It is the men who have been eliminated: men get very short shrift in the book. Is this really the triumph of the 'inner life', or has Forster's plot led him to a conclusion he had not intended?

Chapter summaries, critical commentary, textual notes and revision questions

Chapter 1

The Schlegels have met the Wilcoxes while they were abroad and have been invited to stay at Howards End. Only Helen has been able to go, however. Tibby, the teenage brother, has hay-fever and makes a fuss about it, so Margaret has to stay at Wickham Place to look after him. Helen is enchanted with the house and with the Wilcox family. In the final letter we learn that Helen has fallen in love with the younger son, Paul.

Forster begins characteristically with three letters from Helen to Margaret. This is an excellent device for conveying the maximum information – some of it still rather cryptic – in the minimum space. Helen's letters are breathlessly impressionistic.

Note the casualness of Forster's opening, and the detail which gives the house its distinction. The description is warm and loving, implying a wished-for intimacy. There is revelation too in the immediate effect of the wych-elm on Helen: Helen's impetuosity is the index to her nature, the omissions in her writing even reflecting the way she races at things – and away from them – witness her falling in love. The instruction 'Burn this!' may even convey a certain self-recognition in Helen. The second letter registers her appreciation of Mrs Wilcox, and there is an implicit irony in the fact that it is a man's world, something which Margaret, unaware of at this stage, is later to find out on various levels about Mr Wilcox. The brevity of the third letter is a deepening irony, for there's no instruction to burn this (though in a sense it is the most important of the three). The repetition of 'dearest' shows Helen impetuously confiding and excusing herself at the same time.

Howards End, Tuesday Appropriately enough, we begin with the house that will come to represent all that is most valuable, and threatened, in England.

the dear knows A colloquialism for 'the dear Lord knows'.

gamboge-coloured Gamboge was a yellow pigment. We learn later that Howards End actually belongs to Ruth Wilcox; the male Wilcoxes do not really care for the place; they regard houses as merely bricks and mortar to be bought and sold for profit. So Margaret and Helen had not been so far wrong in imagining the kind of place in which the Wilcoxes would live.

Mr Wilcox bullying porters The Wilcoxes characteristically bully servants and members of the 'lower orders', believing that it is important to keep them in their place. Moreover, they like to get things done.

Men like the Wilcoxes ... a power of good Tibby is, indeed, languidly valetudinarian and could perhaps benefit from a little of the Wilcox backbone. The novel largely concerns the impact of the two families on one another.

Mrs Wilcox ... in the garden ... loves it Ruth Wilcox loves the garden, as she loves Howards End, for itself. The other Wilcoxes think of it as something simply to be used, to play croquet in.

her hands full of the hay ... cut yesterday Mrs Wilcox is a somewhat mysterious figure, a benevolent 'presence'. She is frequently seen in conjunction with hay. It is clearly wrong to ascribe too precise a meaning to these symbols; but she is associated with a natural wisdom and goodness and is rooted in a particular place. In the second letter, her 'steady unselfishness' is referred to. It is notable that the other Wilcoxes and Tibby, but not Margaret or Helen, are allergic to hay.

they are keen on all games The Wilcoxes, with the usual exception of Ruth, are a competitive clan.

having a glorious time. I like them all The letters reveal Helen's vivacity and impetuousness, her quick and impulsive response to people and places. There is also more than a suggestion that her judgement and some of her ideas are uncertain.

horrid things about women's suffrage Women's suffrage was a topical issue. The Schlegel sisters, 'liberated' women, are in favour of it: the Wilcox men believe in masculine superiority, admire 'masculine' characteristics, and find the idea of women voting quite ridiculous.

Chapter 2

Margaret shows Helen's third letter to Aunt Juley, who is staying with her. Aunt Juley believes that it is all 'far too sudden': Margaret is less sure, and is less eager to interfere in Helen's private affairs. However, she determines to go to Howards End to be with her sister at this crisis in her life. Aunt Juley offers to go to Howards End herself; Margaret refuses the offer but, when she discovers that Tibby is quite ill, accepts. She makes the proviso that Aunt Juley must talk only to Helen. When Margaret returns from seeing Aunt Juley off at King's Cross she finds a telegram from Helen saying, 'All over. Wish I had never written. Tell no one. Helen.' But Aunt Juley is irrevocably on her way.

Much of this chapter is given over to necessary retrospect about how Margaret and Helen came to meet the Wilcoxes, and again the climactic note comes at the end with Helen's telegram. We are often told that in a Forster novel nothing happens, but the first two chapters here are redolent of crisis and expectation. Note particularly the imagery of the sea, which conveys the ebb and flow of time and the implication that nothing – not even Wickham Place – is permanent. Mrs Munt reflects the insularity of the English in her remark about the Germans, and her bigotry is shown in other ways, notably in her reaction to Helen falling in love. She is somewhat pompous and self-important, over-protective towards the girls, and snobbish. Margaret reveals a delicious sense of humour, particularly in her 'long engagement indeed' remark. Tibby – the man in the house – is something of a hypochondriac. Margaret shows *her* impetuosity by changing her mind. Forster, like a 19th century novelist, uses his own voice, here in a superbly imaginative paragraph about the London railway stations. The crisis point at the end of the chapter shows Forster having his private chuckle with the reader, something made possible by the confiding tone of the preceding paragraphs.

These, too, would be swept away in time The constant flux of London, the ceaseless building and pulling down of buildings, is something that Forster clearly dislikes; it is the enemy of rootedness and continuity.

Helen isn't a baby Margaret shows characteristic respect for her sister's personality.

no spirit of interference ... make inquiries In Aunt Juley's case there would be no difference between the two.

a profound vivacity ... in her path through life. A key phrase in the depiction of Margaret's nature. The tracing of this response is the main focus of interest in the rest of the book.

Carter Paterson Carter Paterson were a well-known firm of carriers. Margaret's idealism, unlike Helen's, is tempered by realism and healthy self-mockery.

Chapter 3

A chapter of delightfully ironical social comedy, of the kind that is one of the recurrent delights of the book.

We learn that Margaret is eight years older than Helen: Helen is now twenty-one, Margaret twenty-nine. Their mother had died at Tibby's birth, their father eleven years ago.

Aunt Juely loves meddling in her nieces' affairs and is convinced that, unless she preserves them from such a fate, they will 'throw themselves away'. Margaret has, sensibly, twice refused her offers to come and live with them.

At Hilton station Aunt Juley encounters Charles Wilcox, who has been seeing off his father. Because of a misunderstanding over the meanings of the word 'younger', she thinks Charles is Paul. Despite the dust and noise of the car (Charles always kicks up a dust), and the fact that Charles has to stop from time to time to pick up various purchases, Aunt Juley broaches the subject with the man she thinks is Helen's lover. When he realizes that Aunt Juley must be referring to 'some silliness of Paul's', Charles is rude, talking to her 'as if he was talking to a porter'. Soon they are engaged in a full-blown and childish slanging-match, 'Capping Families'. Charles thinks that Paul has made a fool of himself, falling in love when he is in no position to marry, and Aunt Juley resents the slight on her niece. When they reach Howards End Helen rushes out of the house, having just received a telegram from Margaret and hoping to prevent trouble by saying, 'It's over'. Charles confronts Paul aggressively and it needs Mrs Wilcox's calm intervention to cool things down.

Again note the use of retrospect to integrate the characters into the action. Most of the important points in this chapter are covered by the summary above. Mrs Munt's character continues to be spelled out although she is only a minor figure. The interaction with Charles is comic because of the basic misunderstanding initially, but this changes to an over-the-top anger and temper. Already we get the suggestion that Charles has been taken over by the motor-car which in turn is taking over society. You should particularly notice the convincing nature of the dialogue which so accurately reflects the emotional temperature. The crisis note is again sounded at the end of the chapter, but here the symbolic presence of Mrs Wilcox, as well as her factual intervention, conveys peace.

the Deceased Wife's Sister Bill This Bill made it legal for a man to marry his deceased wife's sister. Only before the passing of such a Bill would it have been respectable for Mrs Munt to live in the same house as her widowed brother-in-law. The Bill was passed in 1907 after long debate.

Foreign Things, which always smash Although she may be the leading light of the cultural life of Swanage, Aunt Juley has a deep distrust of all things non-English. Similarly, she distrusts the 'unshaven musicians, an actress even' whom the Schlegel sisters invite to Wickham Place. She is incorrigibly provincial.

the stench of motor-cars ... anti-bilious pills Again Forster, who is constantly present in the novel as a commentator, expresses his distaste for the newly developing 'culture'. He sees the motor-car, then a comparatively new toy, as a stinking, dust-creating agent of hurry and meaningless movement. It is particularly associated with Charles, the dust of whose car enters the lungs of the villagers. Charles's only reaction is, 'I wonder when they'll learn wisdom and tar the roads.'

My time's of value, though yours mayn't be The Wilcoxes
characteristically measure time in financial terms.

disobeying Margaret's instructions ... in the letter Aunt
Juley has some of the Wilcoxes' unconscious dishonesty: like
them, she believes that the end justifies the means.

lower orders vanished in a cloud of dust This is a theme
whose implications are examined and developed in various
places in the novel – for instance in the story of Leonard Bast.

plain question, plain answer Charles typically sees things in
black and white terms: but Mrs Wilcox, who says that there
aren't such things as plain questions, knows the complexity of
personal relations.

**She seemed to belong ... to the house ... overshadowed
it** Again Mrs Wilcox is identified with 'the instinctive wisdom of
the past', with rootedness in a small, particular place, in
opposition to hurry and mere novelty. She is a centre of calm.

They do not love any longer Mrs Wilcox has an intuitive
understanding of the situation. There is even a suggestion of
psychic powers.

Chapter 4

Helen and her aunt return to London in a state of collapse.
When they recover, Helen tells her story to Margaret.

She had fallen in love with the Wilcox family despite –
perhaps because of – the total contrast between the attitudes
of the Wilcoxes and those of the Schlegels. Helen had been
psychologically prepared to fall in love with Paul. To some
extent Paul had merely taken advantage of her, moved by a
momentary impulse, but, however transitory, the experiencce
remains the most intense of her life. On the following morning, when Helen came down to breakfast, Paul had looked
frightened – 'mad with terror in case I said the wrong thing'.
She sees the Wilcox family as presenting 'a wall of news-
papers and motor-cars and golf-clubs and that if it fell I
should find nothing behind it but panic and emptiness'. The
romance ended in embarrassment and Helen sent the
telegram to Margaret; then there was the row when Aunt
Juley arrived. 'To think,' said Margaret, 'that because you

and a young man meet there must be all these telegrams and anger.'

Margaret meditates on the difference between their world, where personal relations are supreme, and the 'great outer life' of business and affairs. There's grit in it,' she says. 'It does breed character.' Later in the book she tries to build a bridge to connect the two worlds which, she thinks, need each other.

We are given a brief account of the Schlegel family history. Their father was German, but not imperialist. When he saw the growth of Germany's power and materialism, he became a naturalized Englishman. He had no patience with the belief of one kind of German that Germany 'was appointed by God to govern the world' – or, for that matter, with British imperialism. He loathed the vulgarity of minds that are impressed by great size.

Bear in mind the epigraph or motto to the novel – 'Only connect', which is vitally important to an understanding of this chapter. The division between the Wilcox–Schlegel ways of life and their different standards is immense. The Forsterian irony embraces the embrace of Paul and Helen and particularly the reactions afterwards of Paul, already conditioned to a role in life. The divisions are emphasized in the dialogue between Helen and Margaret, for Helen's account reveals the lack of common ground with the Wilcox family. The warmth and understanding between the two sisters is apparent and is one of the main character currents running through the novel. Here the retrospect on Mr Schlegel and the decision to become naturalized is of major importance to our understanding of the sisters.

she had *liked* being told that ... Equality was nonsense
... There follows a list of the Schlegel interests and 'fetishes' – Equality, Votes for Women, Socialism, Literature and Art.

If they don't understand it, I do One is reminded of Hamlet's comment to Polonius, who intends to treat the players according to their deserts: 'Use them after your own honour and dignity: the less they deserve, the more merit is in your bounty' (Act 2, Scene 2). Two different notions of morality are involved.

panic and emptiness One of the novel's recurrent phrases or 'leitmotivs'. Panic and emptiness enter the Wilcoxes' lives when emotion appears.

Mrs Wilcox knew How? Mrs Wilcox just *knows* – though it is possible that she overheard something.

telegrams and anger Another recurrent phrase, hardly distinguishable from 'panic and emptiness'.

the things that you can use Compare Helen's comment about the Wilcoxes in her first letter: 'they put everything to use.' The contrast is with the comment at the end of the paragraph: 'But which of them [the mountain of 'facts'] will rekindle the light within?' 'The light within' is a phrase with Quaker associations, and it is interesting that Mrs Wilcox has Quaker antecedents (see Chapter 11).

Eşterház and Weimar Ducal courts which had encouraged musicians and poets.

any human being ... any organization The insistence on the particular and the personal is typical of Forster.

rather apt to entice people ... herself enticed A remark that becomes important in Helen's subsequent relations with Leonard Bast.

Chapter 5

Some time has elapsed. Mrs Munt is again visiting Wickham Place. The Schlegels, Mrs Munt and their German cousins go to a concert in the Queen's Hall. Forster makes wicked comedy about the different ways in which people listen to music. Helen interprets Beethoven's Fifth Symphony in a literary, 'programmatic' way, seeing the last movement as a battle between heroes and goblins. Leonard Bast, at present an unnamed young man, sits alongside them. Helen leaves the concert after the symphony, inadvertently taking the young man's umbrella. The young man, who is desperately trying to acquire 'culture' and is poor enough for such things as umbrellas to be important, fears that the umbrella has been stolen. After the concert Margaret takes the young man to Wickham Place so that the umbrella may be returned. She talks culture as they go, but Leonard is too uncertain of himself – he is bad at pronouncing foreign names – to join in.

At Wickham Place Helen is tactless about the umbrella – such things are unimportant to her – and picks up Leonard's umbrella, saying, 'It's an appalling umbrella. It must be mine.' Leonard flees, to the sisters' distress. The incident is likened to a 'goblin footfall'.

Firstly, note how easily Forster negotiates the passage of time and how naturally he captures the main features of this concert scene. There is a keen insight into the subjectivity involved in listening to music (see summary above) and an equally keen study of a family–friends group. Even thus early, our first introduction to him, Leonard is the outsider, and you might also note Tibby's complete involvement in the music. The sisters are above convention, and Margaret's taking over of Leonard reflects her capacity for goodness – but again 'connection' is difficulty in view of his obvious embarrassment. Leonard has an acute inferiority-complex, as we see in his reactions to the 'cultured' conversation. We register the wit of the girls again, and also Margaret's protectiveness towards Tibby. Culture continues unabated when Leonard has gone.

wunderschöning and prachtvolleying Exclaiming 'wunderschön' (wonderful) and 'prachtvoll' (beautiful).

President Roosevelt Theodore Roosevelt (1858–1919), President of the United States from 1901 to 1909.

To trust people is a luxury in which only the wealthy can indulge Later in the chapter Margaret explains how her father used to say, 'It's better to be fooled than to be suspicious,' and accepted the occasional loss as 'rent'. But the Schlegels can afford to buy more apostle-spoons; Leonard can't afford another umbrella. The value of money in the leading of a civilized life is stressed throughout the book.

An unhappy family, if talented Leonard doesn't understand that in the Schlegel family 'quarrelling' – intellectual argument – is part of the fun.

All is not for the best A reference to Dr Pangloss's insanely optimistic belief (in Voltaire's *Candide*) that 'all is for the best in the best of all possible worlds.'

Chapter 6

The chapter shows us Leonard Bast at home: a dark, stuffy, furnished basement flat in Brixton. His reading of Ruskin's *Stones of Venice* contrasts ironically with his actual surroundings. Ruskin can preach the Victorian virtues of 'Effort and Self-Sacrifice' but he knows nothing of the poverty, dirt and hunger which are the insistent, apparently inescapable, actualities of Leonard's life. Leonard lives with Jacky, who is thirty-three and has once been pretty in a vulgar way but is now descending rapidly into 'the colourless years'. She has inveigled him into promising to marry her when he is twenty-one, which will be soon. Leonard does the cooking; Jacky does nothing. Conversation involves exchanging 'a few statements'. The scene shows us Leonard's pathetic striving for culture and gentility against insuperable odds. Again the importance of money is emphasized: 'his mind and his body had alike been underfed, because he was poor.

Ironic opening to this chapter in the authorial voice, but a superb use of contrast in the description of Leonard's life, with considerable sympathetic insight into his reactions. There is a deadly monotony and lack of inspiration in his existence, and Forster's style, though always tinged with the ironic innuendo ('It was an amorous and not unpleasant little hole') gives enough factual details to underline the nature of Leonard's deprivation. The photograph frame containing Jacky's picture is used symbolically – the spilt blood and the breakage indicating her effect on Leonard's life. Jacky is almost character-grotesque rather than reality, another telling contrast with the Schlegel girls. The descriptions of Leonard's pathetic attempt to gain 'culture' and the reversal of roles – Leonard cooking the poor food – show Forster's sympathy for the many in this study of an individual way of life.

the masterpieces of Maude Goodman Maude Goodman was a popular painter of vulgar and extreme sentimentality.

To see life steadily and to see it whole In a sonnet 'To a Friend', Matthew Arnold says that Sophocles 'saw life steadily and saw it whole'. The phrase became almost a catch-phrase of liberal culture and there are several echoes of it later in the book.

Chapter 7

Aunt Juley, who studies the flats opposite Wickham Place with nosy enthusiasm, reveals the 'unfortunate' news that the Wilcoxes have come to live there. There is much discussion among the ladies about whether Helen has really recovered from the encounter with Paul; Helen assures them that she has. Nevertheless, it is suggested that emotions and interests, once vividly aroused, can never wholly die.

Mrs Munt characteristically tries to make the most of the situation, but Margaret's common-sense carries the day. Interesting is Margaret's revelation that she had written to Mrs Wilcox and had no reply earlier, and also her very favourable comment on Mr Wilcox. Margaret's statements about money – note the imagery she uses – underline this important strand in the novel. The final exchanges between Margaret and Helen show the latter's self-mocking quality and the nature of Margaret's worry underneath. The arrival of the Wilcoxes, though, smacks of some contrivance on Forster's part.

Because I'd sooner risk it The Schlegels are always ready to take risks, but it may be argued that they risk other people's happiness as well as their own.

I stand each year upon six hundred pounds This, of course, was a very considerable income in those days. Margaret is again commenting on the importance of money as a condition of freedom.

Chapter 8

The chapter develops the important relationship between Margaret and Mrs Wilcox. In the previous chapter we learned that Margaret had written to Mrs Wilcox, apologizing for the 'trouble' Helen had caused. Mrs Wilcox had not replied, which Margaret thinks may have been sensible. Hadn't she herself been overcome by 'panic'?

It is suggested that Mrs Wilcox had, at their first meeting in Speyer, detected in Margaret 'a deeper sympathy, a sounder judgement'. Mrs Wilcox now comes to call at Wickham Place. Helen, still asserting that she has recovered from the Paul episode, goes to stay with Frieda in Germany. Margaret writes a letter to Mrs Wilcox saying that, in view of past events, it would be better if they did not meet; she receives a curt reply in which Mrs Wilcox says that she had called to say that Paul had gone abroad. Filled with shame, Margaret rushes across to apologize and their friendship begins.

This marks one of the turning points in the plot, with Mrs Wilcox's visit setting in train the relationship with Margaret. There is some comedy, first in Helen's departure and Tibby eating Elvas plums and later feeling ill. Margaret's initial response is an offence against Mrs Wilcox's sensitivity in calling to give Paul's departure news, but her warm and self-blaming impetuosity in trying to put things right shows her complete lack of conventional observance. Mrs Wilcox resting is a natural preparation for her sudden death – unobtrusive yet effective. The brief news of Charles's wedding is also significant in the development of the plot. Margaret senses intuitively and sensitively the importance of Howards End to Mrs Wilcox. There is pathos in the latter's reference to the way in which the motor-car has taken over from the pony. Forster is of course stressing his own dislike of this modern mechanized age. A vital plot clue is given in the fact that Mrs Wilcox herself owns Howards End, and in her seeing into what she calls Margaret's 'inexperience'.

keine Dame No lady.
Wilcox and Box A facetious reference to the famous farce *Cox and Box* by J. M. Morton (1811–91).
Most certainly her love has died Forster mocks a particular kind of German solemnity.

At Howards End – yes Mrs Wilcox's voice quickens only when speaking of Howards End. Otherwise, 'pictures, concerts and people are all of small and equal value'. Later in the chapter she reveals that she was born at Howards End and owns the house.

built a little one [garage] only last month Only later do we learn that Mrs Wilcox particularly loved the paddock; the building of the garage near the wych-elm is an example of Mr Wilcox's insensitivity.

She ... played with the photograph frame, dropped it, smashed Dolly's glass ... cut her finger thereon... There is a curious and obscure parallel here with Leonard's dropping of Jacky's photograph in Chapter 6. Perhaps the implication is that Dolly is as vacuous as Jacky.

to live by proportion Another version of 'Only connect'.

Revision questions on Chapters 1–8

1 Compare and contrast Margaret and Helen as they are revealed in these first few chapters.

2 Give an account of the Wilcox family, bringing out the characteristics of each of them clearly.

3 Which incident do you find humorous in these chapters and why?

4 Show how Forster uses contrast by comparing any two of these first eight chapters.

Chapter 9

Margaret invites Mrs Wilcox to a 'little luncheon party' to meet 'one or two delightful people', but the party is not a success. Mrs Wilcox has little interest in 'culture' and 'clever talk alarmed her': in view of the samples of clever talk which we are given in the chapter, one sympathizes. The other guests dismiss Mrs Wilcox as uninteresting, but Margaret suddenly feels 'we lead the lives of gibbering monkeys'.

This is another aspect of the Forsterian comedy, with the luncheon party providing the sad evidence of a failure to 'connect'. The cultural references and the ironic play over them means that the emphasis on Mrs Wilcox as symbol – perhaps of sanity, or of something which cannot easily be defined – is emphasized. One wonders if Forster's emphasis on her conveying 'the idea of greatness' is in part a tribute to her quiet courage in keeping her physical suffering to herself. At the same time one is aware of her deprivation – 'We never discuss anything at Howards End' – and the determined and obtuse insularity of her family which Forster is satirizing. At least Margaret becomes more fully aware as a result of Mrs Wilcox's inability successfully to take part in their intellectualism. But the quality of her character, the effect of her personality, is seen in the 'newborn emotion' which all feel when she takes her leave.

the exit into the Baltic ... pianissimo This kind of talk of Helen's is indeed pretentious.

She was not intellectual ... the idea of greatness Mr Wilcox's greatness is a greatness of 'being', which is difficult, perhaps impossible, for a novelist to convey. To a large extent the reader has to accept it, or not, as a datum. It is interesting to compare the portrait of Mrs Moore in *A Passage to India* with that of Mrs Wilcox.

bricks and mortar alone ... cannot stand without them It is typical of Mrs Wilcox to insist on the importance of the physical and the actual.

wiser to leave action ... to men Mrs Wilcox has a gift for producing conversation-stopping remarks. 'Discussion', to her, is mere 'chatter' – a word that she uses towards the end of the chapter.

I'm not particularly well just today Mrs Wilcox's sudden death is, in fact, carefully prepared for in a number of hints; but she keeps her illness to herself, not wishing to trouble her family, who can't live with the idea of death.

Chapter 10

It is several days before Margaret sees Mrs Wilcox again. She is impatient to develop the friendship, but Mrs Wilcox lives by a more leisurely rhythm, observing the 'periods of quiet that are essential to rue growth'.

Then Mrs Wilcox asks her to help with the Christmas shopping. Mrs Wilcox is lost in the rush and vulgarity of the commercial world. Margaret, in the midst of her chatter, mentions her 'new house'. Mrs Wilcox seizes on the phrase and learns that the Schlegels' lease on Wickham Place expires in two or three years' time. To Mrs Wilcox this is a tragedy: 'I do pity you from the bottom of my heart ... Can what they call civilization be right if people mayn't die in the room where they were born?' When she says 'Howards End was nearly pulled down once. It would have killed me,' she obviously means it literally. Impulsively, she asks Margaret to come immediately to Howards End. Too casually, Margaret says that she will come another day. Mrs Wilcox is annoyed, and they part with comparative coldness.

Over lunch Margaret realizes the importance of her refusal and that she will never be asked again. She discerns that Mrs Wilcox 'had only one passion in life – her house – and that the moment was solemn when Mrs Wilcox invited a friend to share the passion with her.' It is always important in Forster's novels for the characters to recognize these crises in personal relations; they are the true crises of the book. Margaret determines to go, hurries across to Mrs Wilcox's flat, finds that Mrs Wilcox has gone away for the night, and rushes to King's Cross just in time to catch her. They are reunited, but before the train leaves they run into Evie and Mr Wilcox, who have returned two days early from their motoring tour of Yorkshire. Characteristically, they have had a crash and it was not their fault. The visit to Howards End has to be abandoned and Margaret is almost forgotten in the Wilcoxes' whirlwind reunion.

This superb chapter brings Margaret and Wilcox into mystical relationship, much of which is conveyed in the summary above. We are aware that Mrs Wilcox – as in the previous chapter – doesn't 'fit': her pace of life (perhaps now in part conditioned by her illness) contrasts with the 'inexperience' of Margaret, who is, of course, much more organized.

Ironically the present which Mrs Wilcox is to give Margaret is Howards End – a deep irony in view of the fact that Margaret is ultimately to have it. Here we note the mystical stress which Forster is giving to Mrs Wilcox. The passion of the latter's insistence that Margaret go to Howards End with her is very moving – we even get the impression that she is living on borrowed time healthwise, and away from her motor-crazy family. She represents the past and its tranquil traditions. Once more the end of the chapter is climactic with movement, raising narrative expectation, splitting Mrs Wilcox from Margaret, and the other side of her inheritance and the obtrusive nature of the family is made almost farcical.

The crisis opened with a message As already indicated, the true crises in Forster are the crises in personal relations, when one person has to be intuitively receptive to the deepest feelings of another. There is a similar crisis later (see the beginning of Chapter 38, p. 295) when Margaret asks her husband if Helen can stay the night at Howards End. Margaret passes her test; Henry fails his.

something worth your acquaintance In fact, Mrs Wilcox gives Margaret Howards End.

a powder-closet in our next house Mrs Wilcox picks out the phrase 'in our next house' from the surrounding chatter.

Backfisch A German term meaning 'baked fish', used of an awkward young girl.

But imagination triumphed Imagination is the discernment and sympathy required to divine people's true needs and deepest feelings.

You are coming to sleep ... You are coming to stop There are overtones in Mrs Wilcox's words. Margaret is to be the second Mrs Wilcox and the actual and spiritual inheritor of Howards End.

Chapter 11

The chapter begins with the kind of surprise of which Forster was fond – 'The funeral was over.' It is some lines before it emerges that it is Mrs Wilcox who has died, though the alert reader will have known immediately. Almost the last words that Mrs Wilcox spoke in the previous chapter, in reply to her husband's perfunctory inquiry about her health, were 'Fit as a fiddle.'

Forster's brand of social comedy soon takes over. Mr Wilcox suffers acute grief and has no way of coping with it except by staying in his room, since the Wilcoxes avoid the personal note in life. His grief is none the less sincere for the fact that, as emerges later, he has been unfaithful to his wife. Charles too feels the death of his mother, but this doesn't stop him from enjoying his characteristic irritation at the inadequacies of other people – the chauffeur and the rector. Dolly is put firmly in her feminine place.

It emerges that Mrs Wilcox had left a brief, pencilled dying note, leaving Howards End to Margaret. Henry Wilcox and Charles form themselves into a committee and persuade themselves without too many qualms that they need not honour Mrs Wilcox's wish. Forster, stepping into the role of commentator, says that the Wilcoxes are not to be blamed, since the bequest was not legal and was contrary to her intentions in the past. But there are two important Forsterian provisos: the bequest was 'contrary to her nature, so far as it was understood by them'– and they had little understanding of her nature; moreover, 'They did neglect a personal appeal.' This last, we feel, is particularly damning.

The summary above conveys the important emphases in this chapter. There is a neatly ironic focus on the local community's view of Mrs Wilcox and her death – with an even neater particularity in the account of the woodcutter's reactions. The contemplation of this blinkered and selfish family is even more ironic – consider the position of Dolly and the insensitive reduction of her. Later, she is to emerge much more positively, riding out Charles's limitations and his disgrace. The upstairs–downstairs interaction which characterizes the family continues over the car with the news of Howards End cunningly interspersed with the important business concerning it. Forster's best irony is reserved for the 'committee' nature of the father–son reaction. His own voice has full play on their decision to 'neglect a personal appeal'.

a sheaf of tawny chrysanthemums It emerges later that Margaret has sent these coloured flowers.

Her tenderness! Her innocence! Mr Wilcox had seen only one aspect of his wife's nature, and Mrs Wilcox had chosen to show him only one side. Her ideas of business and politics seem to him merely charmingly simple-minded, the kind of ideas he would expect of a woman; he has no perception of non-masculine wisdom.

not so much for myself as for baby Mrs Wilcox's desire was not, alas, fulfilled.

dwelt behind it for fifty years A fine encapsulation of Mr Wilcox's character. His face is a bastion behind which he hides.

Chapter 12

This short chapter completes a phase of the action. Margaret is fascinated by the Wilcoxes, as Helen had been, because they are so different from her. She believes that people like the Wilcoxes foster 'such virtues as neatness, decision and obedience' which have 'formed our civilization'. She writes to Helen that their business is to 'reconcile' the unseen to the seen. It doesn't seem to occur to her that Mrs Wilcox appears to have had remarkably little effect on the rest of the family. Mrs Wilcox was completely lacking in missionary zeal.

Helen returns from Germany, where she has had another proposal. Tibby has been sitting an Oxford scholarship and considering whether Oxford would suit him.

Margaret reveals that she has had a letter from Charles, asking her whether Mrs Wilcox had wanted her to have anything. This, of course, is Charles's method of finding out whether Margaret knows that Mrs Wilcox had left Howards End to her. Mr Wilcox later sends Margaret Mrs Wilcox's silver vinaigrette, thus getting the whole matter off his conscience. Margaret thinks this an extraordinarily generous act.

The mystical element is stressed, perhaps in Margaret's thoughts that 'Truer relationships gleamed'. But the Forster irony darkens with Margaret's generous estimate of Charles's motive in writing ('I thought it good of him . . .), and again his own voice is well in evidence about the nature of life at the close of the chapter.

Chapter 13

More than two years have passed. London becomes smellier, noisier, busier, dirtier. The Schlegels – surrounded by 'the architecture of hurry' and millionaire property-owners who regard people's homes as ways of making quick money by erecting 'Babylonian' flats – have to leave Wickham Place. Fortunately, they have the money to buy a new house. Once again money acts as a buffer to protect the family from the hardness of life.

Tibby, down from Oxford, is resisting Margaret's efforts to make him think about finding a job. Margaret, impressed by the Wilcox virtues, thinks it important for a man to have a job, but the ideas of 'work' and 'duty' and the virtues that built the Empire make Tibby groan.

Helen comes in with a highly coloured account of a visit from Mrs Bast, whom she christens, cruelly, Mrs Lanoline. Jacky has been looking for her husband, who has disappeared, and the visiting-card which Margaret had given to Leonard has become a source of contention between them. Helen embroiders her account of her interview with Jacky for her own entertainment and that of her family. Her high spirits have something frenetic about them and make her seem insensitive: it takes Margaret's greater sobriety to realize that 'there's some horrible volcano smoking somewhere', and to hear 'the goblin footfall'.

This is the record of change, and it opens with an authorial dissertation on London. Margaret, insecure because change has come, is somewhat nagging to Tibby, anxious to promote the work ideal which she has acquired. There is some irony here, with Tibby implying that she ought to marry – unknown to them both, marriage for Margaret is not so far away. The recounting of the Jacky episode enables Helen to indulge her capacity for farce – she is something of an actress. Forster also uses a forecasting irony – Margaret thinks that Leonard may be capable of tragedy – and the end of the chapter is mocking of the seriousness of the sisters. The deeper irony is there in the fact that the existence of 'Mrs Lanoline' is going to mean the 'telling of a life where love and hatred had both decayed'.

smelt more strongly of petrol There are many prophetic insights in the book into the direction in which England, and the world, are moving. For a development of these see Forster's remarkable science fiction short story, *The Machine Stops*.

Chapter 14

Leonard Bast comes to Wickham Place to explain Jacky's visit. Margaret soon sums him up: 'the vague aspirations, the mental dishonesty, the familiarity with the outsides of books'. The Schlegels cannot remember their previous meeting. Leonard invents an obviously untrue story to explain his wife's visit, but Helen and Tibby cruelly refuse to allow him to get away with it. Leonard then explains how he had walked all night. The sisters are thrilled by this adventure, though not by his literary reference to Stevenson, Borrow and Jefferies. 'That the Schlegels had not thought him foolish became a permanent joy.' He sensibly refuses an invitation to follow up his talk with them: 'We can never repeat.'

Helen is again instrumental in promoting the comedy about Leonard, though the reader is aware of the pathos and the lack of real 'connection' between the sisters and Leonard. They in fact are cultural snobs, and his reeling off the names of the books which supposedly mirror his own walking experience provokes their contempt. But they are anxious to 'connect', and Leonard's account of his adventure pleases them because he strips it of poetry and romance. At the same time, his own sense of inferiority makes him wish to keep Helen and Margaret as part of a romance which cannot impinge upon his own sordid sense of reality. That reality is seen in the exchange with Jacky. There are some delightful and unexpected turns of phrase in Forster's description of Leonard – 'his head disappeared like a pudding into a basin'.

The Ordeal of Richard Feverel By George Meredith (1828–1909). It contains a description of a night walk through a forest. *Prince Otto*, by Robert Louis Stevenson (1850–94), contains passages in praise of the joys of the open road, and Stevenson's *Virginibus Puerisque* a chapter on walking tours. George Borrow (1808–81) wrote about his mammoth walks; and Henry David Thoreau (1817–62), in *Walden*, praised and described the simple life.

With unforgettable sincerity he replied: 'No.' The honesty of this reply shines through the surrounding 'literariness' and persuades the sisters that Leonard is 'worth saving'.

he tittuped along ... the heart of a man ticking fast Is not Forster – and are not the Schlegels – patronizing towards Leonard Bast?

Chapter 15

The girls go to a female dining-cum-debating club. Leonard's plight enters largely into the discussion (described with comic irony by Forster) about how a dying millionaire should dispose of her money. Margaret is in favour of spending three hundred a year on him, to dispose of as he wishes – a method which Helen ultimately tries.

On the way home they stop to talk on Chelsea Embankment. Mr Wilcox is also there, and joins them when he overhears the mention of his own name. They ask his opinion of how to help Leonard. Mr Wilcox has no idea or interest, but offers them the confidential advice that Leonard should get out of the Porphyrion Insurance Company which will, he says, smash. This advice later proves calamitous to Leonard. Mr Wilcox also says that he has left Howards End, though he has bought two other pieces of property, one in London and the other in Shropshire. Margaret and Helen, who had previously decided not to 'follow up Mr Bast' – Margaret wisely says 'we mustn't play at friendship' – now decide to invite him to tea in order to tell him about the imminent collapse of the Porphyrion.

The debating club sequence is full of Forsterian irony, but it sounds one of the most important themes in the book – money. Forster is critical of 'the female mind', and obviously feels some condescension in terms of the self-seriousness of the debaters. The long arm of coincidence is used by Forster, here with Mr Wilcox hearing the girls' conversation and thus entering their orbit, in Margaret's case, her life. There is a running moral comment in the fact that 'Since his wife's death he had almost doubled his income'. Note how Margaret sees into Mr Wilcox's limitations but does not reject him. His advice about the Porphyrion is an important hinge in the plot. We also register the return of Howards End and what has happened to it at the end of the chapter.

I quite expect to end my life caring most for a place As Mrs Wilcox had done. Margaret's expectation is fulfilled at the end of the book.
taking shares in the lock at Teddington The Thames is, for Mr Wilcox, something to make money out of.
There's noting like a debate to teach one quickness Again, a characteristically utilitarian remark. Debates are still defended on the grounds that they teach people to lie convincingly.
We employ people because they're unemployed The exchange neatly and wittily encapsulates the difference between the business and the personal approach to things, with the advantages and drawbacks of each.
It's outside the Tariff Ring An alliance of Insurance Companies who would be likely to help and support one another.

Chapter 16

Leonard comes to tea with the Schlegels. He is ill-at-ease. They ask him about his work. Leonard feels that this is prying into his private life while he is 'itching to talk about books'. He thinks of Wickham Place as an oasis of Romance in the desert of his life. Helen reveals that they have heard that the Porphyrion is 'no go'. Leonard, who knows nothing about the commercial condition of the company, denies this.

Mr Wilcox, Evie and two puppies burst in and Leonard tries to get away, saying, truthfully, 'I knew it would be a failure.' The sisters, perhaps foolishly, try to persuade him to stay, but Leonard cries, 'I don't want your patronage.' They remind him of his night-walk, which Evie finds amusing, and Leonard goes out, humiliated, pursued by Helen, who wants to make 'the noodle understand'.

The Wilcoxes completely misunderstand the situation. They think that Margaret and Helen have been *trying* to humiliate Leonard and congratulate them on their success. When Margaret explains the situation, Mr Wilcox says, 'You must keep that type at a distance . . . They aren't our sort, and one must face the fact.' This sort of attitude is unadventurous – the Schlegels like to take risks – but the course of the book proves it not to be untrue.

This is one of the major action scenes of the novel. Leonard is pathetic in his attempts to succeed socially with the girls through his clichés. His reaction to the supposedly suspect nature of the Porphyrion is natural, reflecting his defensiveness. We are aware of the need to pretend (not connect) in this kind of conversation. At the same time, we feel some sympathy for Leonard, who is injured by the interrogation. The interaction with the Wilcoxes, and particularly with Mr Wilcox, is admirably handled. Forster is showing that 'only connect' is at this stage an impossibility between the classes, and the individuals who represent those classes. As Mr Wilcox says to Evie, 'I am really concerned about the way those girls go on'.

a giant, in the classical style Porphyrion was a mythical giant.
What is the good of your stars and trees . . . if they do not enter into our daily lives? This is another of the connections,

between the 'imaginative', the 'poetic' and the 'spiritual', and the 'physical', the 'mundane' and the 'everyday', which Margaret tries to make.

Revision questions on Chapters 9–16

1 Describe in some detail the relationship between Margaret and Mrs Wilcox.

2 Consider the effect of Mrs Wilcox's pencilled note on her husband and Charles.

3 What do you find (a) humorous and (b) sad in the presentation of Leonard and Jacky in this part of the novel?

4 In what ways are Helen and Mr Wilcox totally different in character? Do you find any similarities between them?

Chapter 17

Margaret is unsuccessfully house-hunting. She has to bear this burden alone, since she gets no help from Helen and Tibby. She receives an invitation from Evie Wilcox to dine with her and her fiancé at Simpson's in the Strand. Later she suspects, since Mr Wilcox also appears, that Mr Wilcox had in fact planned the encounter. The strain of trying to find a house, and the sense that comes over her, when she meets the newly-engaged Evie, that 'the vessel of life' is slipping past her, may be factors that help prepare her to accept a proposal of marriage from Mr Wilcox.

The chapter is written mostly from the consciousness of Margaret and her increasing worries about moving and finding the right place. The lunch at Simpson's is another turning point in the narrative, since Evie's behaviour reveals to Margaret her own sense of failure, a hint that Forster is presenting her as developing beyond 'the foolish virgin'. She certainly develops more in the presence of Mr Wilcox, seeing the lovers from a more genial perspective. Forster's comic art encapsulates a conversation which covers the common-place of food, astral bodies, and Margaret (ironically, in view of Mrs Wilcox's bequest) wanting to rent Howards End. Margaret knows that she and Mr Wilcox are drawing closer to each other.

Fancy coming for fish pie to Simpson's Mr Wilcox likes to take charge in every situation, and Margaret isn't unwilling to have her mind made up for her.

We merely want a small house with large rooms and plenty of them Margaret is, of course, conscious of, and amused by, the contradictoriness of her desires.

Chapter 18

The Schlegels have gone to Swanage to stay with Aunt Juley. A letter arrives from Mr Wilcox saying that he has decided to give up his house in Ducie Street and is willing to let it to them, on condition that Margaret comes to London immediately. Margaret wonders whether this is a manoeuvre to get her to London in order to propose to her, but later puts this down to 'feeling solitary and old-maidish'. When she gets to London, Mr Wilcox does, indeed, propose in his stammering way: 'He desired comradeship and affection, but he feared them.' Margaret is filled with an immense and indescribable joy at the proposal and promises to reply by letter when she gets back to Swanage.

The formative chapter in this phase of the plot. Note the inherent deception in Mr Wilcox – Margaret is summoned nominally to consider the house in Ducie Street but really so that Mr Wilcox can propose to her. His uncertainty is reflected in his irritability. We feel the essential complacency of the man beneath this situation – not so much in regard to Margaret but in regard to his secure status in life. Nonetheless the tour of the house means that Forster can indulge his humour at the Wilcox tone ('Here we fellows smoke'). And he shows his command of the inward responses by a fine description of Margaret's feelings in silence at the end of the chapter.

It was as if a motor-car had spawned A remarkably vivid and suggestive picture of the kind of furniture Mr Wilcox would like.

Chapter 19

The chapter begins and ends with paragraphs about the beauty of England; they are obviously deeply felt, but over-written. Aunt Juley, Frieda Mosebach (now Frau Liesecke) are waiting, looking down on Swanage, for Margaret's return. There is an amusing 'international incident' in which the German girl is heavily humourless and critical and Aunt Juley typically insular.

Margaret arrives, driven up from the station by Tibby. She tells Helen about the proposal she has had. Helen bursts out in tearful opposition to the idea of such a marriage; for her, all the Wilcoxes promise 'panic and emptiness'. Margaret admits that she doesn't yet love Henry Wilcox and says that her marriage will be 'prose', unlike Helen's affair with Paul, which was 'Romance'. Indeed, she sums up Henry's faults lucidly and frankly: 'He's afraid of emotion. He cares too much about success, too little about the past. His sympathy lacks poetry, and so isn't sympathy really ... spiritually, he's not as honest as I am.' All of these limitations are to prove true, and crucial, at the crisis of the book. She expresses her appreciation for those practical men of affairs without whom 'you and I couldn't sit here without having our throats cut ... there would be no trains, no ships to carry us literary people about in ... just savagery'. Through her marriage she hopes to make a 'connection' between the two worlds.

On the surface it is obviously true that Henry is more 'spiritually dishonest' than Margaret is, but Margaret may well be ignoring her own desire to 'manage' other people. The gallant attempt to make connections needn't involve marrying unsuitably. One feels that Margaret's common sense has deserted her – or that Forster has had to make it desert her in the interests of his plot.

The authorial tone is poetic in description of the English terrain, but the effect is to hold up the narrative just when we had been expecting it to move. The exchange between Aunt Juley and Frieda is meant to convey the particular prejudices of each. Helen enjoys being sarcastic about the Wilcox ability to collect property, but it is ironic that she should say 'The Great Wilcox peril will never return' when, in an intimate form, it is about to do so. When it does, Helen's reaction shows her hysterical nature, but the exchange between the sisters here is deeply moving, with Margaret rational and considering, Helen emotional and, one feels, afraid for the future. The concluding paragraph, rich in the Forster poetics, turns to another contemplation of landscape, contrasting implicitly with Margaret's inward self-examination.

the island will guard the Island's purity till the end of time In view of the book's general pessimism about the physical fate of the country, it seems that Forster has lapsed into vague sentimentalism.

The Great Wilcox Peril will never return It is, of course, on its way.

Chapter 20

A chapter of delightful irony as Margaret and Henry are played off against each other. We are told that 'Good humour was the dominant note in her relations with Mr Wilcox.' There are, no doubt, worse bases for matrimony, but there may well be times when good humour is not enough. Henry reveals that he has been talking about Greece with Tibby; Margaret congratulates him on the tactful choice of subject but does him too much credit: Henry was merely telling him that he has shares in a currant farm near Calamata! Henry, whose life centres round the making of money, is reluctant to talk about it (though the first evening of their engagement has to be spent in a business talk); he is close about his income, and pretends that he is a poor man, though we have learned earlier that he is nearly a millionaire. Now that he is not trying to sell Ducie Street to Margaret he reveals that it has a mews behind it; earlier, his business mind had unconsciously suppressed this information. If Margaret had been trying to sell the place, her innate honesty would have compelled her to admit, even emphasize, its drawbacks. Ducie Street, he says, is going downhill. Unlike Margaret, he doesn't regret this; he likes continual change, which 'shows things are moving. Good for trade.' As he takes Margaret home he clumsily, without tenderness or prelude, kisses her. 'She had hoped for some interchange of gentle words. But he had hurried away as if ashamed.'

By the end of the chapter they have agreed to marry in September, shortly after Evie's marriage to Percy Cahill.

Notice the heavy personifications in the opening paragraph which perhaps ironically mirror the heavy concerns of Mr Wilcox. Typically, because he feels safe by so doing, he wants to talk business with Margaret. Business consists of being seen to be fair to the rest of his family (the irony being, among other things, that he says that Charles will have Howards End). Margaret reveals her own scarcely submerged hankering for the place. Part of the comedy rests on the interaction with the youths – Mr Wilcox representing the authoritarian upper orders who naturally quell rebellion, even if it's only verbal.

If he was a fortress she was a mountain peak ... whom the snows made nightly virginal What chance has a marriage between two such people? Forster presumably intends us to conclude that Margaret was frigid.

Chapter 21

In the previous chapter Henry Wilcox had said, 'I am determined that my children shall have no case against me,' and

Margaret, who could certainly never be accused of being grasping, had said, 'Be generous to them. Bother justice.' However, it is not surprising that Charles should see in his father's proposed marriage a financial threat: 'Miss Schlegel has fairly got us on toast.' He takes it out on poor Dolly, blaming her for introducing his sister Evie to Cahill instead of allowing her to go on looking after their father – and thereby keeping his mind away from the possibility of remarriage. The dialogue excellently captures Charles's crudely blinkered mind and leaves us in no doubt that in certain circumstances this mind could express itself in crudely physical action.

Charles's reactions are readily predictable, but Forster again makes comedy out of a situation with Dolly seeking refuge in the child as antidote against her husband's childish behaviour. This is described as an 'interlude' by Forster, with the last lines of the chapter a brilliant – and of course ironic – summary: 'Nature is turning out Wilcoxes in this peaceful abode, so that they may inherit the earth.'

Nature is turning out Wilcoxes ... so that they may inherit the earth According to the Beatitudes it is the meek who shall inherit the earth, but meekness is not a Wilcox characteristic. In the end, however, it is Leonard Bast's son who inherits Howards End. Note that Charles produces, prolifically, 'editions' of himself.

Chapter 22

The chapter begins with a statement of what Margaret is trying to achieve in marrying Henry Wilcox: she wants to 'help him to the building of the rainbow bridge that should connect the prose in us with the passion'. But it is stated even at this early stage in their arrangements that she failed because of Henry's 'obtuseness'. He 'simply did not notice things'. He is incapable of subtlety or even insight in any of life's personal relations. This has already been amply illustrated and one would have thought that a woman of Margaret's insight would have seen it already.

Henry casually reveals that the Porphyrion is 'not a bad business', though earlier he had advised that Leonard should leave it because it was in financial danger. Leonard has accepted the advice, passed on by the Schlegel sisters, and has taken a job in Dempster's Bank at a reduced salary. It may well be that Henry is not to blame, since he gave the advice in good faith; but he disclaims responsibility far too easily and casually, saying that it is all part of 'the battle of life', and lectures Helen on the dangers of taking up 'a sentimental attitude over the poor'. But Helen's personal concern is surely right – she says that 'a man who had little money has less, owing to us.' Henry likes to think of life not in terms of people but of great impersonal forces.

Again, he wants Margaret to go up with him to see Howards End on the following Wednesday. Margaret does not want to curtail her annual holiday with Aunt Julcy, who takes great care to entertain them, and will be hurt. Margaret goes as far as to say, 'I won't go. Don't bully me,' but he merely steam-rollers through her objections.

From the ironic opening right through this chapter we are aware of the obtuse nature of Henry Wilcox and wonder whether Margaret is capable of surviving this ever-present insensitivity. Note how perfectly Henry's own concerns dominate the conversation, and note too the structural device of having the two letters mentioned with their different importance to different people. Helen is still resistant to the idea of Margaret's marriage. In essence it is property versus people, with Henry showing his lack of sympathy – or even interest – over the move of Leonard Bast to Dempster's. The wych-elm becomes the symbol of Howards End and its mystical power for Margaret, who finds herself defensively trying to reason with Helen over her (Margaret's) future husband's mistake. Henry ruins any chance of reconciliation with Helen by his pompous and self-justifying pronouncements on business and life. There is no chance of 'connection'. The prose will not be brought into harmony with the passion.

What a rum notion! Of course not! Henry, characteristically, has never heard of the pigs' teeth which were so important to Mrs Wilcox.

the battle of life Successful men are fond of referring to life as a battle, which is far away from the idea of life as 'harmony'.

it's absurd to pretend that anyone is responsible personally Henry and his kind will always deny personal responsibility.

Chapter 23

The chapter opens with a talk between Margaret and Helen. Although Helen doesn't like Henry and can't pretend to, she says to Margaret, 'Go on and marry him. I think you're splendid. And if anybody can pull it off, you will.' She regards Margaret's forthcoming marriage as a heroic enterprise, a brave attempt to 'keep proportion'. With considerable self-knowledge Helen says, 'I can only entice and be enticed. I can't, and won't, attempt difficult relations' – though she doesn't obey the resolution. Margaret is reassured that their relationship is firmly enough grounded to the 'inner life' to be secure, and it does indeed prove to be the firmest thing in the book.

Margaret goes to the offices of the Imperial and West African Rubber Company, where Henry works. Henry, typically, is dictating a 'strong' letter and is full of indignation. He and Charles, who manages to be reasonably polite to his future stepmother, are full of 'telegrams and anger' at the behaviour of Bryce, the tenant of Howards End. Margaret and Henry are driven to Hilton. Margaret hates the speed of car travel: 'Did not a gentleman once motor so quickly through Westmorland that he missed it?' They lunch with the empty-headed but amiable Dolly before going on to Howards End. Henry drives off because he has forgotten the key, but Margaret finds the door open and goes into the deserted house. (There are overtones here, too: Margaret is the 'real' owner and so finds easy entry: Henry has excluded himself.) Margaret looks round and is greeted by the aged and mysterious Miss Avery, who mistakes her for Ruth Wilcox – 'In fancy, of course . . . You had her way of walking.'

This is a character study of Helen, showing degrees of tolerance and idealism. Margaret's visit to the Company shows that she has ventured into a man's world, and her compassion for the decamping tenant of Howards End is wasted on Charles and Henry. The motor-trip is a further emphasis of the divisions, with the Forster tone clearly on Margaret's side: the implication is that these journeys are a waste because there is no time to appreciate the quality of England through its various counties. Margaret's exploration of Howards End involves detailed and loving association and description. As mentioned in the summary, the 'connection' between Margaret and Mrs Wilcox is established through the symbolic figure of Miss Avery, who 'connects' the prose of the present with the passion of the past.

If Drayton were with us again Forster is referring to the English poet, Michael Drayton (1563–1631). The 'incomparable poem' referred to is *Poly-Olbion*, a vast work which takes the reader on a tour of everything of topographical and antiquarian interest in Great Britain. It is, I am assured, full of nymphs, but is not compulsory reading for students of *Howards End*. Sabrina was the nymph of the Severn.

It heaved and merged like porridge The description of the journey gives an excellent picture of Margaret's disorientation.

Chapter 24

We learn some details about Miss Avery. To Henry Wilcox she is 'just one of the crew at the farm', but she has been connected with Howards End for a long time; she had been friendly with Charles's great-grandmother, who had left the house to Mrs Wilcox. Mrs Wilcox had had a brother, or an uncle, who had proposed to Miss Avery. Miss Avery represents continuity at Howards End.

Before they rush back to London Margaret is shown round

the house. She is particularly impressed by the 'peculiar glory' of the wych-elm. She notes that there are, indeed, pigs' teeth in the wych-elm.

The snobbery of Henry is well brought out in this chapter, which sets Miss Avery firmly in context and emphasizes tradition, the 'connection', very strongly. Dolly proves to have a reasonably obvious but also quite endearing sense of humour, something she needs if she is to survive living with Charles, one feels. It is very significant that both Margaret and Henry will not mention Mrs Wilcox's name.

It gave her quite a turn It didn't, of course; but Henry has his stereotype of the female sex to which he makes the facts conform.
There you stood clutching a bunch of weeds Like Mrs Wilcox.
Take it as a rule that nothing pays on a small scale Economically, Henry may be right; but the Schlegels believe that all things of real value are on a small scale.

Revision questions on Chapters 17–24

1 Describe the effect of Mr Wilcox's proposal on
(a) Margaret and (b) Helen.

2 In what ways does Forster display his irony towards the making of money in these chapters?

3 What does Margaret learn of Henry's character after she has accepted his proposal?

4 Indicate the roles played in this section of the novel by Charles and Miss Avery.

Chapter 25

The chapter begins with Evie's childish and absurd resentment of her father's engagement – though it is hard that she should be blamed for it by Charles and Dolly. Her wedding is put forward to August.

Margaret has to play her part at the wedding. It will be an

opportunity for her to get to know Henry's 'set' — who are not a likeable lot, since Henry takes no care over the choice of his friends. The wedding is to take place at Oniton.

Margaret travels from Paddington to Shrewsbury with a party of Wilcox friends: Charles is to meet them with no less than three cars at Shrewsbury. Helen has refused her invitation; Tibby hasn't troubled to answer his. Henry has organized the journey efficiently, though Charles's efficiency at Shrewsbury is bossy and impatient.

The car in which Margaret is travelling, driven by Albert Fussell, runs over a cat. The ladies are disembarked and put in the car behind, and Charles drives them on. A girl screams: Charles makes light of it; Margaret insists that she wants to go back. Mrs Warrington believes that a little money will put the matter right: Margaret thinks that it needs a woman to look after the matter; she jumps out of the slowly moving car, hurting herself. Charles finds himself in the unusual position of having 'a woman in revolt' on his hands. Albert Fussell arrives, having left the chauffeurs to deal with the situation. Charles tries to console Margaret with the thought that it wasn't a dog, as he originally thought, but 'only a rotten cat'. The chauffeurs appear, announcing that all is well since the girl will receive compensation for the cat.

The incident shrewdly shows up the Wilcox world: its indifference to the feeling of others, particularly those of the 'lower classes'; its dishonesty; and its belief in the power of money to solve all problems. Moreover, Charles completely misunderstands Margaret's reaction: he thinks that she has merely panicked in what he believes to be a typically feminine way. However (and this is another important aspect of the incident), Margaret allows Charles's version of what happened — that she had been a victim of female 'nerves' — to go unchallenged: she doesn't want Henry to be troubled with her Schlegel scruples, the subtlety of which he is too stupid to understand. She is compromising; and it seems a strange way of trying to persuade him to see the light.

Charles concludes that Margaret is a dangerous woman, with a 'tongue', and believes that she is in a conspiracy with Helen and Aunt Juley to rob him and the other Wilcoxes of their rightful inheritance.

The narrow-mindedness of Evie is meant to typify the blinkered and totally selfish attitudes of this philistine family (with the exception of their dead mother). There is some humour in the fact that 'her play went simply to pot' when she is told of her father's forthcoming marriage. She and Charles are small-minded. The essential superficiality of Henry's 'set' is spelled out. Oniton represents Henry's own lack of real acuteness, judging from the disadvantages which are listed – that is, disadvantages by his standards. The lack of connection is made even more apparent by Helen and Tibby not being there, so that we understand that Margaret is the agent of connection with an uphill task. Forster is always liable to produce the dramatic incident, and the one here is made so by Margaret's reactions – again they show her distance from those with whom she must now consort. Forster is at once condemning the omnipresence of the motor-car and the insensitivity of Charles and his kind. There is some superb irony, as ever, in this chapter, with Charles feeling that Margaret will disgrace his father (in fact, of course, Charles himself is to do just that). Even more obtuse – or vain – is his idea that Margaret is perhaps in love with him.

womenfolk reported the scenery as nothing much Scenery, of course, is regarded as something to be left to the ladies.
Tariff Reform The proposal to increase the tariff on goods imported from countries which were not in the British Empire.

Chapter 26

The day of Evie's wedding. Margaret likes Oniton, particularly the marvellous view. She thinks that it will be her home and doesn't know that Henry is planning to sell it. Forster makes fun of the fuss and bother which Charles makes over such a simple thing as going for a bathe; he can't bathe without his 'appliances' and things are never to his satisfaction.

Margaret arranges an 'interview' with her future husband – it is best to make an appointment with him. She is impressed by the enormous extent of her future responsibilities when she becomes mistress of Oniton. The wedding goes well – that is to say, without incident – though Margaret, when she sees what a complicated and expensive feat of organization a society wedding is, becomes anxious about her own wedding. As she says, her aunt is not 'used to entertainments on a large scale'. She is relieved when Henry says that the arrangements should be left in the hands of an hotel.

Helen unexpectedly bursts in on the aftermath of Evie's wedding, furious and in her oldest clothes. She has brought the Basts with her. She has discovered that Leonard has lost his job in the bank and that the Basts are 'starving'. 'We upper classes have ruined them,' she says with fierce sarcasm, 'and I suppose you'll tell me it's the battle of life.' Margaret's feelings are mixed: she is angry with Helen for her apparent hysteria and for bursting in at Oniton on Evie's wedding-day, yet she is sympathetic towards Leonard. Leonard is depressed and fatalistic. He has lost his job and knows that it is almost impossible for somebody in his position to find another one. Helen is determined that Henry Wilcox shall undo the harm he has done, by offering Leonard work. Margaret promises that if Helen will take the Basts to the local hotel, she will speak to Henry. She leaves the Basts tucking in to the ample remains of the wedding breakfast.

Margaret speaks to Henry, using the 'methods of the harem' to persuade him to see Leonard: she is conscious that she is giving him 'the kind of woman he desired'. They find Mrs Bast still in the garden, drinking champagne – Helen and Leonard have gone to engage rooms. Jacky is clearly drunk, but she recognizes Henry. She has had an affair with him ten years ago. Henry releases Margaret from her engagement.

Margaret realizes that, as the episode took place ten years ago, 'it is not her tragedy: it was Mrs Wilcox's.'

At this stage, Forster makes no comment, but lets events speak for themselves. Margaret's reactions are left until later.

The humour here is at the expense of Charles and his fussiness, but Margaret's liking Oniton in ignorance of Henry's intentions is yet another instance of the failure to connect. The satire of the wedding preparations is direct, but it is a measure of Margaret's conformity – or is it compromise? – that she allows herself to scream with the others. We are aware that the motor-car is now part, a major part, of conventional observance – Margaret is not allowed to walk to church. Helen's capacity for drama in the forefront of her idealism is here carried to the highest pitch. By a strange contrast, she is as bossy in her own way as Henry is in his. The production of the Basts is a melodramatic stroke, but there is friction between the sisters as a result, and following this, a condescending Henry agrees to see Leonard. Event follows event in this quick-moving chapter, and Margaret's real lack of experience is shown in her naive attitude towards Jacky recognizing 'Hen' before the latter enlightens her about the true state of past affairs. This is given a further twist by Henry believing that Margaret has deliberately engineered the confrontation of Jacky in order to humiliate him. The last words of the chapter are masterly in their brevity *and* the expanse of time which they cover.

She knew why not, but said that she did not know Margaret
   presumably thinks that Henry's kind of chivalry involves a
   degree of superiority and condescension.
a Durbar The levée of an Indian prince or an Anglo-Indian
   governor.
He discountenanced risqué conversations now Times have
   changed since it was thought 'risqué' for a woman to use the
   word 'drunk'!
**Allow me to congratulate you on the success of your
   plan** Henry is accusing Margaret of a carefully contrived piece
   of blackmail. Surely this is the supreme insult.

Chapter 27

Helen discusses with Leonard – more accurately, she lectures him on – the Wilcox inability to admit personal responsibility. There is something condescending in Helen's attitude towards the Basts (of which she is at least half aware), so that she doesn't allow him to suggest criticism of Mr Wilcox.

Jacky, who is now in bed, has told Leonard about her past relationship with Henry Wilcox. Leonard is determined to preserve Helen, and Margaret for Helen's sake, from the knowledge. He doesn't realize that Margaret already knows. Helen asks Leonard about Jacky. Leonard says, touchingly, 'I needn't have married her, but as I have I must stick to her.' He reveals that his family have disowned him because of Jacky's past and admits, with shame, that he comes from a family of agricultural labourers. Helen's reaction to Jacky's past is, 'I blame, not your wife for these things, but men.'

Leonard has lost his interest in music, books and the pursuit of culture. Understandably, he now believes that 'the real thing's money, and all the rest is a dream.' Helen tries to console him and to persuade him to 'never give in' by urging that 'the idea of Death' shows the emptiness of money. It is not surprising that, for Leonard, 'Death, Life and Materialism were fine words, but would Mr Wilcox take him on as a clerk?'

Notes arrive for both of them from Margaret.

Helen's lecturing of Leonard underlines the essential bossiness of her nature – she loves taking over. Leonard is naturally reticent about his wife's past, but one wonders if Helen and Leonard really 'connect' in the sense of understanding each other. Helen is really subjecting Leonard to an interrogation. When she gets onto the subject of Death we are aware too, I think, that she is listening to the sound of her own voice. But this sequence is charged with irony in view of the fact that Death is to be a reality as a result of the manoeuvring and interference from Helen – Leonard's death at the hands of Charles, but life too with the birth of Helen's baby.

Pierpoint Morgan An American financier who collected large numbers of paintings.

Death destroys a man; the idea of Death saves him Helen thinks that the fact that we know we are going to die alters our system of values. She may well be right, but she has chosen a bad moment to say so.

Chapter 28

Margaret, her feelings deeply bruised, writes to Henry saying 'this is not to part us', but her heart is not in this simple answer; she can't so easily pretend that nothing of importance has happened. 'Men must be different, even to want to yield to such a temptation.' She tears up the letter. She then writes a note to Leonard saying that Mr Wilcox cannot help him. Clearly it is impossible in the new circumstances. She writes to Helen saying, rather brusquely, that 'the Basts are no good' and asking Helen to come round at once and spend the night at Oniton. She wants to avoid a dangerous meeting between Helen and Jacky. She delivers the notes in person at the hotel. When she returns she meets Henry, but nothing is said about Henry's affair with Jacky.

Before she goes to sleep – because she loves him, because she pities him and because she hopes to change him – Margaret determines to go through with the marriage. After all, she reflects, considering the kind of man Henry was, there was likely to be a Jacky in his past. Much of this is difficult for the reader to swallow.

The sequel to this scene does not appear until Chapter 40. Forster keeps it as a surprise for the climax of his novel, and, incidentally, avoids the necessity for direct description. Helen thinks that Margaret's letters have been written at Henry's dictation and are the last touch of his callousness. She extracts from Leonard the story of Jacky's liaison with Henry. In loneliness, pity and indignation she has her half-hour of love with Leonard.

Margaret in a divided frame of mind has recourse to letters

– a natural reflex in view of the difficulty of speech after Jacky's revelation. The concentration on Margaret's consciousness is a cunning device by Forster – it takes us away from the coming together – the temporary, sexual 'connection' between Leonard and Helen which leads to the climax of the novel.

Chapter 29

The following morning Margaret talks to Henry. He is incapable of true repentance and has to 'improvise emotion'. Deprived of his 'fortress' of respectability, he hides by making himself out to be a 'bad lot'. The fact that he had been unfaithful to Ruth, which to Margaret is the important point, never occurs to him. As Forster later remarks (Chapter 31), Ruth had never found him out. Henry tells her the story – it had happened in Cyprus – and Margaret 'plays the girl', helping him to rebuild his fortress.

Margaret visits the George and finds that Helen and the Basts have left, but not together. Margaret guesses that Helen must have heard the story of Henry and Jacky.

Henry realizes that he has laid himself open to blackmail, and Margaret knows that if necessary he will deny that he had ever known Mrs Bast.

They leave Oniton. Margaret has grown already to love the place, but she will never see it again.

Margaret's connection with Henry shows her capacity for adjustment and reveals his abject lack of depth or real identity – something which she has to accept, and to build her life with him despite her doubts (which she has put down). Thus Margaret herself endures a kind of deprivation. She convinces herself that she loves him, but the uncertainty of her position is symbolized by her standing in the car to look over Oniton which she loves, seeing her future life with Henry. Forster's dry comment (of Oniton) is 'She never saw it again'.

Chapter 30

Helen visits Tibby, who is in his last year at Oxford, 'glancing disdainfully at Chinese'. Helen has 'the look of a sailor who has lost everything at sea'. She says that she is going abroad and bursts into tears while Tibby goes calmly on with his lunch: 'He had never been interested in human beings.' Helen says that Henry Wilcox has ruined two people's lives – Jacky's and Leonard's, though it seems likely that Jacky had been 'ruined' earlier. She doesn't know whether Margaret knows about Henry and Jacky, and whether she should tell her. She leaves the decision to Tibby, who will always do nothing, if possible. She also decides to give five thousand pounds to the Basts as 'compensation', since nobody else will help them.

The next day Tibby is summoned by Margaret, who is worried by Helen's sudden departure and discovers that Helen does indeed know about Henry's past affair. She writes to Helen.

Tibby sends a cheque for the first hundred pounds to Leonard, who returns it, saying that he doesn't need help. Tibby sends Leonard's letter on to Helen, who replies, frantically, that he is to go to Leonard and compel him to accept the money. Tibby goes, but finds that the Basts have been evicted for not paying their rent and nobody knows where they have gone.

This is a chapter of clever contrasts, with the focus initially on Helen and her 'look of appeal' which of course Tibby does not understand. Her hysteria is a sure index that she is unhappy, and her going abroad a deliberate clue as to what has happened. Once again her reactions with regard to the money are over the top. Margaret's reactions are natural, but there is certainly misunderstanding about the real reason for Helen's flight. We feel now a degree of narrative tension.

Mods The first part of the Classical course at Oxford.
She stopped like a frightened animal Helen is alarmed at the impetuousness and possible hysteria of her visit to Oniton. She seems to be wondering, herself, if she is perhaps not quite sane.

Chapter 31

Margaret moves from Wickham Place, which has been demolished. Henry offers Howards End as a warehouse for her furniture, and the Schlegels' goods are 'entrusted to the guardianship of Miss Avery'. Henry and Margaret are married quietly and spend their honeymoon near Innsbruck. Margaret hopes to meet Helen, but Helen avoids her. Margaret concentrates on being a submissive wife: Henry regards any departure from submissiveness as feminine 'nerves', as when he suddenly and casually reveals, to her annoyance, that without consulting her he has sold Oniton. They will live in Ducie Street for the winter and look for another place in the spring. In contented domesticity Margaret loses interest in cultural matters. She is passing from 'words to things'.

The first paragraph on the death of Wickham Place is moving and personalized, perhaps underlining Forster's own fear of change. With the removal of the furniture it is true to say that Margaret already has Howards End – which she is finally to have anyway – since it has become the repository of Schlegel possessions. After the marriage and the exchange of letters we feel the misunderstanding that exists between the two sisters – Margaret is really pleading for Henry when she asks for 'charity in sexual matters'. This is another failure to connect, since it is Helen (unknown to Margaret) to whom charity needs to be extended. Significantly, Forster mentions Margaret's 'bad attack of nerves during the honeymoon', an indication perhaps of the sexual (and social) strain she is under. The real state of her situation is shown in her annoyance at the sale of Oniton, and her ironic remark that it 'must be inhabited by little boys'. Forster however mentions a certain growth in Margaret as a result of her experience, for 'she was passing from words to things'.

Helen thanked her for her kind letter Ironical. Helen, of
  course, is pregnant, though the reader hasn't yet been told this.
Had he only known that Margaret was awaiting him ... he

would have kept himself worthier of her This, of course, is
utter hypocrisy and self-deception; and he has forgotten Ruth.
Wedekind or John Frank Wedekind (1864–1918) was a
contemporary German dramatist and Augustus John (1878–
1961) a fashionable British painter, born in Tenby, Wales.

Chapter 32

It is the following spring, and Henry has decided to build a
house in Sussex. Dolly bursts in to see Margaret; she has been
sent by Charles, because Miss Avery has been unpacking
Margaret's possessions at Howards End. Charles angrily sees
this as a deliberate takeover attempt by Margaret, and has
sent Dolly to find out what is going on. Dolly is supposed to
say that of course Margaret doesn't know about it, but in her
goodheartedly scatter-brained way she says first one thing,
then the other. Margaret determines to go to Howards End to
see for herself.

Dolly, whose chatter is an important source of news for
Margaret, reveals that Miss Avery had sent Evie an expensive
wedding present. The Wilcoxes, who believe in keeping servants in their place, see this merely as an attempt on Miss
Avery's part to secure an invitation to the wedding, and the
present is returned. Margaret suggests that Miss Avery may
have given Evie the present in remembrance of her mother.
This is a new idea to Dolly, but she is more generous than her
menfolk and accepts the possibility.

Charles is in some financial difficulty; he is even having to
sell his car, the ultimate disaster. Henry has not, in fact, been
generous to him, though Margaret is urging him to give a
larger allowance.

The revelations of Dolly mark another important movement in the plot, and the conversation is a mixture of superficiality and oblique cross-reference – 'Yet another baby was
expected' being Dolly's, though with Forster's careful chron-
ology of Helen's time abroad – 8 months – a clue is being laid
as to Helen's state too. The snobbery of the returned present is

repugnant. The climax of Margaret deciding to go to the house (which is morally and sympathetically hers) closes the chapter and leaves the reader with a sense of expectation.

Chapter 33

Forster begins with some – perhaps unnecessary – meditations on the landscape and on the absence of an English mythology. At times he teeters on the edge of whimsy.

Miss Avery's niece takes Margaret to Howards End. At first they receive no answer, and the eccentric Miss Avery refuses to appear until her niece has gone away. She has clearly been expecting the new 'Mrs Wilcox'. Margaret finds to her amazement that Miss Avery has furnished Howards End with her furniture from Wickham Place, which fits very well. Miss Avery's explanation is that 'the house is Mrs Wilcox's and she would not desire it to remain empty any longer'. She also prophesies that Margaret will come back soon to live at Howards End. Margaret is amused and puzzled (not surprisingly) by Miss Avery, who seems to distinguish imperfectly between the first and the second Mrs Wilcox. At one moment she seems a 'maundering old woman', at another 'she looked capable of scathing wit and also of high but unostentatious nobility.' Margaret determines to store her furniture elsewhere and consults Henry, who advises her to store it in London.

The leisurely opening to the chapter perhaps contributes to this sense of expectation. Margaret and Miss Avery's niece leave the farm, their way to Howards End drawing forth from Forster some whimsical and poetic description. The eccentricity of Miss Avery is stressed – in some ways she complements *the* Mrs Wilcox –, but she also acts as prophet when she tells Margaret that *she* (Margaret) will live at Howards End. The fitting of the furniture is again prophetic – it reinforces Miss Avery's idea that this Mrs Wilcox will come to Howards End. Despite Margaret's determination to move it, we feel in this chapter perhaps more than any other the power of the place – the draw, the sympathetic affinity, the spiritual and mystical associations which are as real as living reality. Margaret duly consults Henry about the furniture, but we know what he will say. Forster is an adept at rousing expectation, as we see from the end of the chapter once more. But it turns out that the 'trouble' is perhaps not what we expected: Forster's comic technique involves conning the reader from time to time, as here.

she who walks through the myrtles of Tuscany Botticelli's Primavera.

the maidy The meadow.

There's not one Wilcox that can stand up against a field in June By contrast, Mrs Wilcox was constantly seen with a wisp of hay in her hand. Is the other Wilcoxes' susceptibility to hay-fever intended to represent their difference from Mrs Wilcox?

Revision questions on Chapters 25–33

1 Write a critical account of Chapter 25, bringing out the difference between Margaret's world and the world of the Wilcoxes.

2 Which do you find the most dramatic incident in this sequence and why?

3 Indicate the part played by Howards End itself in these chapters. In what way do you feel it is important to our understanding of particular characters?

4 Write a character study of Henry Wilcox, basing it on what you learn of him in these chapters.

Chapter 34

Aunt Juley falls ill with pneumonia. Margaret and Tibby go down to Swanage, and Helen is telegraphed for. Helen replies that she can only stay until Aunt Juley is out of danger; then she must return to Germany. But before she can get to London Aunt Juley recovers.

Margaret is deeply pained by Helen's persistent absence and odd behaviour. She writes little and Margaret's attributes the estrangement to Helen's dislike of Henry. Margaret thinks that Helen's behaviour is morbid and traces it back four years to her meeting with Paul: she thinks that Helen is reacting against the Wilcoxes to such an extent that she is scarcely sane.

Helen writes an odd letter saying that she will not come to Swanage if Aunt Juley is better or if she is dead. She also asks where their furniture is, since she wants to pick up some books. Margaret is tempted to reply that Aunt Juley is still in danger – in this way she would be able to see Helen – but her natural honesty wins and she replies that her aunt is much better. Helen sends a telegram asking for the address of the furniture and saying that she will return abroad immediately. Margaret wires, 'Certainly not; meet me at the bankers at four' and goes to London with Tibby. Helen is not there and they can find no trace of her. Genuinely fearful that something may be the matter with Helen's mind, for Helen never 'sins against affection', Margaret consults the 'practical' Henry.

When Henry can be brought to view the matter seriously – he is at first inclined to dismiss Helen's behaviour as typical of the odd Schlegels – he suggests that Helen is sent to Howards End to look for her books and that Margaret, without Helen's knowledge, goes to meet her there. And 'there'll be a motor round the corner, and we can run her up to a specialist in no time'! Margaret at first refuses to practise this piece of deception, which implies distrust of her sister, but eventually gives in. She writes to Helen saying that the furniture is at Howards End and that the charwoman will let her in at three o'clock on the following Monday. She is thus reduced to ambushing her sister.

The opening is a fine piece of atmospheric writing about Aunt Juley's garrulous state during her illness, but we feel that the main concern is Margaret's worry over Helen's sanity and what is happening to her at the moment. There is some superbly ironic writing when Tibby and Margaret go up to London – 'The mask fell off the city, and she saw it for what it really is – a caricature of infinity'. With Helen being in England but refusing to see them, the mystery deepens, though one feels that the obvious explanation eludes Margaret and Tibby because of their impractical natures.

Si monumentum requiris, circumspice 'If you want to see his monument, look around you.' Sir Christopher Wren's epitaph.

Chapter 35

When they arrive at Hilton, Henry discovers that Helen is already at Howards End. Seeing how distressed Margaret is, he tries to slip off on his own and tackle Helen in his own way [it would have been an interesting encounter!], but Margaret forestalls him. She does not reproach him because 'he was only treating her as she had treated Helen, and her rage at his dishonesty only helped to indicate what Helen would feel against them'. Henry has the ambush planned like a military operation. They pick up the local doctor. Henry discusses Helen's 'case' with the doctor, labelling her in a way that Margaret deeply resents. She is tempted to say that there is nothing wrong with her sister, 'though she did resent my husband's 'immorality'. She knows that she must be on her sister's side. 'They would be mad together if the world chose to consider them so.'

Helen is visible when they reach Howards End, sitting in the porch. Margaret jumps out of the car and runs up the garden path, shutting the gate in her husband's face. She sees that Helen is pregnant. She unlocked the house and thrusts Helen inside.

This brief graphic chapter shows how Forster handles the crisis of the plot: Henry and Margaret establish scant connection, and his attempt to leave her behind (when her own sister is involved) shows just how insensitive he can be. Margaret's own excitable reactions show that in some respects she is like Helen, but her presence of mind in pushing Helen into the house is admirable.

Chapter 36

Margaret is determined to get rid of the men, particularly the doctor, Mansbridge. She feels that she is fighting for 'women against men'. Mansbridge finds out from the driver of Helen's carriage that Helen is pregnant and tells Henry, who is of course appalled. Margaret is roused to her old self, which can be formidable. 'It all turns on affection now,' she says. 'I like Helen very much, you not so much.' She adds – for she is no longer the submissive wife – 'For one sensible remark I will let you in. But you cannot make it.' Eventually Henry goes away.

Another brief but telling chapter – Margaret roused to defence and to positive action. The obtuseness of Henry has never been more apparent. And always there is the feeling that he fears the spread of gossip. In one sense this is Margaret's finest hour.

My darling, forgive me Margaret is asking forgiveness for having deceived her sister. Contrast Henry's characteristic reactions to situations.

Chapter 37

Helen is deeply hurt that she has been deceived; she even asks bitterly whether Aunt Juley has really been ill. Margaret doesn't rebuke Helen for her pregnancy; she doesn't even ask any questions. She feels that *her* crime, absence of confidence, is greater than any crime Helen may have committed. Helen feels that she can never live in England again, since she has done something which 'England can never pardon'. She is living in Munich with Monica, an Italian feminist who will see her through. There is constraint between the sisters – 'both suffered acutely, and were not comforted by the knowledge that affection survived' – and there seems nothing for it but for Helen to go away.

Forster then beautifully dramatizes the thawing out of their icy awkwardness. It is the only true love scene in the book. The surroundings of their furniture brings back shared memories of their childhood, when Tibby spilt the soup – or was it coffee? – over the chairs, and so on. Helen becomes more like her old self, 'irresponsible and charming'. A small boy, sent by the vigilant and prophetic Miss Avery, calls to offer them milk. The 'wonderful powers' of Howards End have begun to operate. Helen conceives the idea that they should spend the night together there. She has become 'the Helen who had written the memorable letters four years ago'. Margaret is very tempted, but knows that 'Charles wouldn't like it'. But in response to Helen's 'I see little happiness ahead. Cannot I have this one night with you?' she goes off to speak to Henry. She is disquieted, because Miss Avery's prophecy that she would soon be spending the night at Howards End is coming true.

This is a remarkable chapter of reconciliation, with Margaret's honesty and self-recognition confronting all those respectable deceptions which we practice in life. Helen's turning to a feminist – Helen who in her own time has been much courted – underlines the extent of her loneliness. But she has come through to a new sense of recognition herself (she no longer hates Henry), but she sees the impossibility of coming back into Margaret's life. The delivery of Henry's message ('domestic French') shows how anxious he is to cover up the situation. The reference to the sword shows Forster structuring the narrative – here it is 'Magnificent', but it is to be the implement of death. There is a fine anticipatory passage which speaks of hope for them both – 'And all the time their salvation was lying round them – the past sanctifying the present; the present, with wild heart-throb, declaring that there would after all be a future, with laughter and the voices of children'. The mystical and positive effect of Howards End has registered on the two sisters. It is perhaps epitomized in Helen's recognition 'This is ours. Our furniture, our sort of people coming to the door'.

Chapter 38

Henry deals with the 'problem' item by item, as is his custom. He shows no sympathy towards Margaret or Helen, nor does he stop to wonder whether they have any feelings about the matter. He even imagines that 'this is far worse for me than you', since the difficulty, as far as he is concerned, lies in discussing such unpleasant matters with his wife at all. 'Was your sister wearing a wedding-ring?' and 'I am obliged to ask you the name of her seducer' are the questions on his agenda. The only thought in his mind is that the seducer must be made to marry Helen and her 'name' saved. Charles has already been informed and has gone to see Tibby, the male member of the Schlegel family. Margaret is so incensed at Henry's insensitivity that she says, 'But suppose he turns out to be married already? One has heard of such cases.' Her point, of course, is that Henry, as a married man, has also seduced a young girl, but Henry is too stupid and walled in self-righteousness to see the connection, and Margaret is thankful for it since their whole relationship would have been imperilled. Henry merely answers, in the conventional language of the Edwardian gentleman, 'In that case he must be thrashed within an inch of his life.'

Margaret then puts her request. May Helen stay the night at Howards End? It is the crisis of Henry's life. He *has* to see the importance of the request and be generous. She regrets that, in her anger, she has not led up to the question more carefully, so that he might have been warned of its import-ance, which he is quite incapable of seeing for himself. He weighs it 'like a business proposition' and finds various objections, particulary when he learns that Margaret intends to spend the night there too. Henry refuses: he cannot answer a personal appeal. 'I have my children and the memory of my dear wife to consider,' he says as though Helen's condition might 'depreciate the property'. He is a canting humbug. Margaret, who has been controlling herself, lets herself go and mentions Mrs Bast, determined that Henry shall 'see the connection'. 'You have had a mistress – I forgave you. My sister has a lover – you drive her from the house.' With fine eloquence she drives home his faults and blindness, trying to get beyond his 'fortress'. But Henry is impenetrable. 'The two cases are different,' he says, applying the double standards for which men are notorious in such matters. He falls back on accusing Margaret of trying to blackmail him.

Forster's explicitness at the beginning of the chapter kindles our expectations. The conventional reactions of Henry show how little he and Margaret connect. The divisions between them cannot be healed by marriage, for Henry – like his son Charles – is incapable of change. Margaret's will to confront him with his own modes of deception in the past merely emphasizes the distance. The main points of this chapter are covered in the summary above.

dwelling on the hateful word thoughtfully Margaret doesn't
know whether Helen has been seduced or has a more permanent
lover.
thrashed within an inch of his life Were seducers ever
thrashed within inches of their lives? I lack information on the
subject.

Chapter 39

Charles visits Tibby in Ducie Street. Tibby is the man of the family and therefore, in theory though not in practice, the appropriate person to deal with. Charles is convinced that the whole sequence of events has been a conspiracy, a campaign by the Schlegel sisters to get hold of Howards End. He thinks that Helen is a most dangerous family foe, and is determined to get rid of her before she disgraces them further. He blusters and bullies, and Tibby, to his later shame, reveals the name of the Basts.

Charles in English indignation confronting Tibby who lives in a different world, about Helen's situation, succeeds in getting his own way to the extent that the revelation about the Basts sets off the train of events which leads to Charles being imprisoned. The irony therefore plays over the coming fact of poetic justice.

Chapter 40

An elegiac chapter in which Helen and Margaret talk, and later sleep, in Howards End. They are lapped in its peace. It is Helen's evening and Margaret says nothing about her own tragedy, the failure of her marriage. Helen tells a little of the story of her love-affair with Leonard. As we learn in the next chapter, 'she loved him absolutely, perhaps for half an hour.' She asks Margaret to come and stay with her in Germany, but it is not the time for making plans.

This chapter considers in some depth the question of individuality which cannot be grouped under particular penalties or laws. There is an exquisite pathos in Helen's confession (if that is the right word) about her affair with Leonard – 'Oh, Meg, the little that is known about these things'. Margaret is sustained by the inner knowledge that Mrs Wilcox understands their situation. But she feels another kind of reality with regard to Henry – 'She had just as soon vanish from his mind'.

Christ was evasive when they questioned Him When the woman taken in adultery was brought to Jesus, he said, 'Let him who is without sin among you be the first to throw a stone at her' (John, 8,7).
I feel that you and I and Henry are only fragments of that woman's mind It is difficult to know what to make of remarks

like this, or of the question that closes the chapter. One cannot simply reject them as Margaret's passing fancies, inspired by the moonlight and the intimacy of the occasion, since they belong to a vein of mysticism that runs through the whole book.

Chapter 41

The chapter follows Leonard's development from the night at Oniton to his death. His overwhelming feeling is remorse. He blames himself, never Helen, whom he idealizes. He refuses the money Helen offers, but he still has to live. He becomes a professional begger, sponging on his family. He becomes increasingly tender towards Jacky, reflecting that 'there is nothing to choose between us after all'. One day he sees Margaret in St Paul's – she has called in on her way to consult Henry about Helen – and conceives a desire to confess to Margaret. Moreover, he might get news of Helen, which would be the 'supreme reward'. By hanging around Mr Wilcox's office he finds out that Mr Wilcox is married. Eventually he finds his address. On the day when Henry and Margaret have gone to Howards End to ambush Helen, he goes to Ducie Street. The parlourmaid tells him where they have gone. That night, unable to sleep, he takes the train to Hilton and enters Howards End at breakfast-time. Charles is there. Somebody (Margaret, in fact) calls Leonard's name. Charles embarks on his 'gentlemanly duty' of thrashing him within an inch of his life, using the Schlegel sword which hangs in the hall, and accidentally kills him. The arm of coincidence is somewhat overstretched in these events.

This is a chapter of retrospect on Leonard up to his death at Howards End. Since it deals with the 'facts' of his existence, it lacks the intensity of the previous chapters, and its close seems to be melodramatic. There is much on Leonard's consciousness, but Forster's entry into it is not as convincing as it has been with Helen and Margaret. It is significant that Miss Avery has the final word, which epitomizes her mystical quality and the ultimate truth: Charles may have killed accidentally, but his attitude to 'lesser' humanity is a murderous one.

And if I drink oblivion of a day The words come from George Meredith's *Modern Love*.

Six forest trees ... grow out of one of the graves in Tewin churchyard The legends of the trees and of the hermit actually exist.

A stick, very bright, descended The old German sword is an appropriate weapon to use in 'an affair of honour'. It may also suggest a degree of Schlegel responsibility for Leonard's death.

Books fell over him in a shower Leonard is submerged under the 'culture' he had so ardently sought.

Chapter 42

The action moves back in time to Charles's arrival in Hilton after seeing Tibby. Margaret is missing. She has disobeyed. After midnight Henry tells Charles the story of Helen's desire to spend the night at Howards End, omitting, of course, any mention of Mrs Bast, and insisting that no quarrel took place. He insists, too, that Margaret and Helen must be removed, emphasizing the 'rights of property' which he prefers to more human rights. Charles offers to go early in the morning to carry out the congenial task of evicting them.

The following day, when Charles returns from Howards End (having first called in at the police station to report Leonard's death), he tells his father his version of the story. 'They had the man up there with them, too.' The implication is that Helen, with Margaret's connivance, had been carrying on her 'affair' at Howards End. Charles passes as lightly as he can over Leonard's death: 'there is no need to trouble about the man. He was in the last stages of heart-disease' and he had merely caught him once or twice over the shoulders with the sword. Margaret has sent a message, 'with love', that she is going that evening to Germany with Helen.

Charles is anxious about the future. The police will ferret out the story of Helen and Margaret and he will be unable to continue living at Hilton, the scene of such a scandal. Henry goes to the police station – does he go to try to influence the police or to get a true account of the facts? – and returns to say that there will be an inquest on the following day, which Charles is required to attend. Charles has no sense of guilt: he merely thinks that he will be 'the most important witness there'.

The main interest in this chapter is the one-sided version of events which Charles gives – he is even full of self-importance about appearing at the inquest. Little or no thought is given to Margaret or Helen or the dead man, and this is a further indication of the self-centred natures of father and son. It is ironic that Charles thinks he may not be able to live at Hilton because of the scandal involving Helen, whereas in fact he is to supply all the local scandal when he is imprisoned.

the talent in the napkin The reference here is to the words of St Jerome (Eusebius Sophronius Hieronymus – c.342–420), in his *Letters*, 14,8: 'Woe to the man who receives a talent and ties it in a napkin.' Doubtless St Jerome was thinking of the worthless servant in the parable of the talents (Matthew, 25,24–30) and in the parable of the pounds (Luke, 19,20–26).

Chapter 43

Margaret feels that they have all been caught in the machinery of cause and effect and that they have lost their true selves. She is questioned about Leonard's death and says that 'Mr Wilcox may have induced death, but if it wasn't one thing it would have been another.' The doctor confirms – honestly, presumably – that the death was due to heart-disease. Helen stays at the farmhouse for the night.

Margaret is still determined to go to Germany with her sister. No message has come from Henry and 'she neither forgave him for his behaviour nor wished to forgive him'.

Henry sends Crane, the chauffeur, for Margaret. Margaret tells Henry that she is leaving him. She returns the keys of

Howards End. Henry says that the verdict at the inquest will be 'Manslaughter' and that Charles may be sent to prison. 'I'm broken. I'm ended.' Charles is, indeed, sent to prison for three years. Henry's 'fortress' finally gives way. He can bear nobody near him but Margaret and asks her to do what she can with him. She takes him up to Howards End.

The focus here is on the strong individuality of Margaret in adversity. The distance between herself and Henry has now widened. Their meeting is adroitly (and of course ironically) handled by Forster ('The Great North Road should have been bordered all its length with glebe. Henry's kind had filched most of it'). Note the economy of the style, the balance of 'heart-disease' and 'manslaughter': Margaret is emotionally blackmailed in taking Henry back to 'her' house, Howards End.

No one ever told the lad he'll have a child Miss Avery is the only one who seems to spare much thought for Leonard. There is no mention of Jacky's fate, for which the Wilcoxes and Schlegels are surely responsible.

Chapter 44

Helen's baby is one year old. Fourteen months have passed. It is hay-making time. Tom, the small boy who had brought the milk to Howards End, plays with the baby. They have all settled at Howards End for good. Henry is indoors, still suffering from hay-fever, and now 'eternally tired'. Margaret says, 'He has worked hard all his life and noticed nothing. Those are the people who collapse when they do notice a thing.' Helen has come to like Henry. She is forgetting Leonard and is grieved to think that love itself has been a dream. Margaret tells Helen not to fret herself but to accept herself as she is. She makes a plea for tolerance towards differences in human beings and ways of life. 'Develop what you have. Love your child.' After Charles's arrest she has patiently nursed her two invalids, Henry and Helen, and built a new life. They have a sense of London creeping to the very edge of Hilton; from where they sit they can see the 'red rust'. 'Life's being melted down, all over the world.' But Margaret feels that Howards End, with its peace and stability, may be the basis for the future.

Inside the house there has been a family conclave to which Margaret is summoned by Paul. Paul has returned to England to manage the business and seems to have turned into a very unpleasant young man. Henry has been disposing of his property and has left Howards End, but no money, to Margaret. Margaret, in turn, intends to leave the house to her nephew. Dolly, nervous and tactless as ever, reveals that Ruth Wilcox had left Howards End to Margaret and now Margaret has got it after all. When they have all gone, Margaret asks Henry about this and Henry tells a very selective version of the truth. Helen bursts in, carrying the baby and holding Tom by the hand, and ends the book by announcing that the meadow is cut and there will be a record crop of hay.

This marks the passage of time and the register of change. Howards End, the legacy of Mrs Wilcox, is the salvation of lives which are beginning, or are changed or are broken. There is some 'connection' in the fact that Helen has come to like Henry. She has also achieved a fuller appreciation of her sister, who has come to Howards End and been the most important influence on their lives (the authorial implication would connect her with Mrs Wilcox). Dolly, as earlier, gives the game away. Margaret shivers at the duplicity, but assumes her usual attitude towards her husband, who has always been unequal to the truth.

Tom wants to know whether baby is old enough to play with hay The baby seems to have Ruth Wilcox's attitude towards hay even at his tender age: perhaps this is a hopeful sign!

You and Henry learned to understand one another Forster seems to be manipulating a 'happy ending' here: Henry is surely incapable of understanding Helen, and Helen has always understood Henry only too well. The end of the book makes it clear that he is still the same old humbug; and in any case it is an essential feature of his character that he is incapable of change.

Revision questions on Chapters 34–44

1 In what ways does Margaret show her strength of character in dealing with Helen? What light does this shed on her relationship with Henry?

2 Describe in some detail Henry's reactions to the situation.

3 Do you find Charles's actions convincing, or do you find the killing of Leonard too contrived? Give reasons for your answer and quote in support of your views.

4 What do you feel about the last two chapters of the novel? Do you feel that this is the right ending (a) from the moral point of view and (b) from the artistic point of view? Again, give reasons for your answer.

The characters

Margaret

Margaret is the central character in the novel and the most completely drawn. She is the centre of consciousness in nearly every scene. In Chapter 2 Forster sums her up and sums up the cause of her fascination: she has 'a profound vivacity, a continual and sincere response to all that she encountered in her path through life' (p. 25), and the author is nearly always able to rise to the challenge of that description.

She is not young: at the beginning of the novel she is twenty-nine. Nor is she beautiful: she is toothy and rather angular. Like her sister she is 'emancipated', interested in ideas and in the arts. She has an inherited private income of six hundred a year in the days when money went a long way, and is very aware of the importance of money in the pursuit of the good life. Like her sister, she values personal relationships above all else.

But, unlike Helen, Margaret is not an extremist: she sees other point of view and is able to laugh at herself. Early on, when Aunt Juley wants to go to Howards End to ask questions about Helen's 'affair' with Paul (Chapter 2, p. 25), Margaret prevents her and says, 'If Helen had written the same about a shop assistant or a penniless clerk ... or if she had wanted to marry the man who calls for Carter Paterson, I should have said the same.' Then she adds, 'Though in the case of Carter Paterson I should want it to be a very long engagement indeed, I must say.' She believes in trusting people, not because such a policy necessarily brings the best results but because one owes it to oneself to act in that way.

She soon comes under the influence of Mrs Wilcox, who is alarmed by the clever talk to which Margaret and, more particularly, her friends are prone. Mrs Wilcox thinks it 'wiser to leave action and discussion to men'; and she loves the continuing life of Howards End. As time goes on Margaret becomes increasingly identified with Mrs Wilcox; she becomes the new Mrs Wilcox and comes to own Howards End. And, while still remaining Margaret, she also takes over much of Ruth's wisdom and quietude of spirit.

Unlike Helen and Tibby, Margaret sees and values the Wilcox virtues – 'neatness, decision and obedience, virtues of the second rank, no doubt, but they have formed our civilization ... they keep the soul from becoming sloppy' (Chapter 12, p. 112). She sees the dangers to which her kind are subject, of becoming sloppy, effeminate and ineffective, and refuses to despise the practical men without whom 'you and I couldn't sit here without having our throats cut'. So she accepts Henry's proposal of marriage. There are signs that she fears becoming an old maid – though one would have expected her to bear such a fate with humour and equanimity; indeed one might go further and say that she was cut out by Nature to be an old maid. Certainly she likes Henry, but she understands his weakness and analyses them with such clarity that Helen says, understandably, 'You must be mad.'

Both Schlegel sisters have a missionary spirit and Margaret wants to *change* Henry, to make him see the light and make the connection between the poetry and the prose – the Schlegel world and the Wilcox world – whose separation she sees as the chief problem of her time. She is unperturbed by the thought – it seems not even to occur to her – that even Ruth Wilcox seems to have had no effect on Henry. The desire to change a man is not the best reason for marrying him.

Some critics have regarded Margaret's marriage to Henry as unlikely, a transparent piece of plot-manipulation on the author's part. One ought to remember that when a novelist's characters and actions are completely explicable and consistent it is generally because there is not much to know about them: it is only in detective stories that people have completely simple 'motives'. Needless to say, people *do* make extraordinary marriages. Nevertheless, the criticism seems just. It is very difficult to know whether Forster intended us to think of Margaret's marriage as an aberration on her part – apparently not, since he seems to approve of the experiment. Forster doesn't seem to realize what an unattractive man he has created in Henry. It isn't as if he reveals himself gradually; he is a blinkered humbug from the start, yet we are expected to take on trust that he is in some way attractive.

Despite the fact that Margaret subdues herself to be a submissive wife and shows truly heroic patience, her plan – and therefore her marriage – fails. Henry is too stupid and too dishonest to see the connections between things.

The most permanent part of Margaret is her love for Helen, which is rooted in 'common things'. She lowers her colours, it is true, by agreeing to Henry's plan to ambush Helen; but she does so out of love and anxiety, and because she does not possess Helen's absolutism. The delicacy and honest and uncensoriousness with which she treats Helen is very moving. Margaret can be very formidable, and her denunciation of Henry's hypocrisy and double standards, when he refuses to allow Helen to stay at Howards End, is devastating.

At the end Margaret is left as the presiding genius of Howards End. By patience and devotion she has pulled Henry through, though he is little more than a shell, and in her relationship with Helen the 'inner life' has truly paid, even though the experiments in connection have brought nothing but disaster, in the short term at any rate.

It is a tribute to the power of Forster's presentation of Margaret that she cannot be easily summed up. The reader has to watch her in her subtle responses to each situation as it arises.

Helen

Helen has much in common with Margaret but she is more beautiful, more impulsive, idealistic and uncompromising.

We are told that she 'was rather apt to entice people, and, in enticing them, to be herself enticed' (Chapter 4, p. 44) – a remark which casts much light on her relationship with Leonard Bast.

She falls easily in love with Paul – or, more accurately, with the whole Wilcox family – and equally quickly out of love. Because of the Wilcox reaction of 'panic and emptiness' she conceives a deep, obsessive hatred of all the Wilcoxes, which is confirmed and exacerbated for her by Henry's casual indifference to the fate of Leonard Bast and to his responsibility for it.

Unlike Margaret, who simply listens to the music, Helen translates Beethoven's Fifth Symphony into a story of goblins, gods and demi-gods. She is quickly imaginative; she talks too much and too often without thinking. All her responses to life are intense, excitable and exaggerated. Apart from her short meeting at the beginning of the book she does not come under the influence of Mrs Wilcox. Margaret remarks shrewdly of her: 'Helen is too relentless. One can't deal in her high-handed manner with the world.'

She can be tactless and thoughtlessly cruel. She prattles on about her habit of stealing umbrellas, taking no account of Leonard's feelings; later, she refuses to allow Leonard to get away with his explanation of Jacky's visit. After Leonard's description of his night walk, Helen, like her sister, is genuinely touched by him, though there is something smugly patronizing about both sisters' desire to help him and their tendency to discuss him as a 'case' rather than as a human being.

Helen's wrath is really aroused by Henry Wilcox's attitude towards Leonard. Leonard leaves the Porphyrion Insurance Company on Henry's advice and joins Dempster's Bank at a reduced salary (which Helen characteristically describes as a *greatly* reduced salary). When it emerges that the Porphyrion is soundly based after all, Helen is livid. She is particularly angry that Henry sees the misfortune as the inevitable result of the working of impersonal economic forces and refuses to acknowledge personal responsibility. Her sympathy for

Leonard is genuine, like her determination to see the matter in personal terms — 'a man who had little money has less, owing to us' — but she is also in psychological need of a 'cause' into which to throw her energies. Moreover, the 'cause' gives a focus to her dislike for the Wilcoxes and all that they stand for. It is hard not to believe that she is *using* Leonard as a weapon with which to beat the Wilcoxes.

When Leonard loses his job in Dempster's bank, Helen takes violent action. She sweeps down to the Basts, pays the rent, redeems the furniture, feeds them and *orders* them to meet her at Paddington the next morning. Leonard's views are ignored. She takes them to Shropshire to confront the Wilcoxes, bursting in on the day of Evie's wedding, to which she has refused an invitation. She is 'dominated by that tense wounding excitement that had made her a terror in their nursery days' (Chapter 26, p. 222). Margaret regards such behaviour as 'theatrical nonsense' and begins to wonder if Helen is mad — a fear that grows during Helen's later un-explained absence. She also accuses Helen, justly, of being self-indulgent.

Helen lectures Leonard, inappropriately in the circum-stances, on the unimportance of money, yet later tries to give him five thousand pounds — taking up, as is her wont, extreme yet contradictory positions. She sleeps with Leonard out of a variety of emotions — loneliness, pity, a desire to identify herself with the downtrodden; disgust at the vulgar trappings of Evie's wedding.

Later, when she meets Margaret again at Howards End, she becomes — under the influence of their common experi-ence, memories and possessions — more like the old Helen again, irresponsible and charming. It is difficult to believe, however, that she would ever have found it possible to like Henry, and she seems to be too easily able to accept her part in Leonard's fate.

Tibby

Tibby is a beautifully drawn comic miniature. He is intelligent but languidly idle, 'dyspeptic and difficle'. His enjoyment of art is genuine, but inclined towards preciousness – he listens to Beethoven's Fifth with the full score open and draws everybody's attention to 'the transitional passage on the drum'. He wants 'civilization without activity' – a happy state to which he is able to aspire because of his substantial private income – and he moans and bleats at Margaret's insistence that he should think about finding a job. During the discussion about the possibility of his working for a living he 'leant so far back in his chair that he extended in a horizontal line from knees to throat'. He goes straight from adolescence to middle age, by-passing youth. He is 'untroubled by passions' and 'had never been interested in human beings'; he is incapable of anger, shock, or any dynamic human emotion beyond idle curiosity. Forster perhaps shows more sympathy towards him than Tibby deserves, since his slothfulness is not merely physical but emotional and spiritual too.

It is worth adding that Margaret, Helen and Tibby are all different, yet obviously related. It is an excellent portrait of a *family*.

Henry Wilcox

All the Wilcoxes 'avoided the personal note in life'. Henry has strong feelings – he is genuinely distressed by Ruth Wilcox's death – but they are submerged. He has built himself inside a 'fortress' and when the fortress is broken down he collapses completely. 'He never bothered over the mysterious and private.' Margaret says, 'I know all Mr Wilcox's faults. He's afraid of emotion. He cares too much about success, too little about the past. His sympathy lacks poetry, and so isn't sympathy really. I'd even say that, spiritually, he's not as honest as I am' (Chapter 19, p. 177).

He is good at making money and, though he describes himself as a poor man, he is almost a millionaire. He is constantly buying and selling property – houses, to him, are something to be developed and sold at a profit. He turns Howards End into a warehouse and regards beauty as something for women only. His interest in Greece is limited to the fact that he has shares in a currant farm there. He is one of those who are the cause of the constant flux, of the 'melting down of life all over the world', which distresses Margaret and Mrs Wilcox. He says, 'Shows things are moving. Good for trade.' Margaret values him as one of those who have created our civilization, but he is also in danger of making that civilization intolerable to civilized people. He would not have understood Ruth's question, 'Can what they call civilization be right, if people mayn't die in the room where they were born?'

He is used to having his own way and, unlike the Schlegels, can never admit that he is wrong. His attitude to everything is utilitarian: the value of a debate is to 'teach one quickness'. His dishonesty is unconscious; he rewrites the truth to suit his own convenience. In small matters this is merely comic – as when, trying to sell Ducie Street, he omits to mention the fact that there is a mews behind it. In more important matters his dishonesty stems from a mental and moral obtuseness. He is simply unable to see the connections between things. When his affair with Jacky is revealed it never occurs to him that he has offended against Ruth; after all, she didn't find him out. His contrition is contrived. He is sorry only that his front of respectability has been disturbed. Expelled from his old fortress he has to build himself a new one around the fact that he is a bad lot; and he has soon persuaded himself that 'had he known that Margaret was awaiting him he would have kept himself worthier of her'. He builds his life on this kind of lie.

He is incapable of noticing the double standards he applies to life. He is furious at Helen's affair with Leonard, but sees no connection between that and his own affair with Jacky, which is, indeed, a great deal more sordid. Not even Margaret's eloquent indictment gets through to him: 'You have had a mistress – I forgave you. My sister has a lover – you drive her from the house ... stupid, hypocritical, cruel ... a man who insults his wife when she is alive and cants with her memory when she's dead ... and gives bad financial advice and then says that he is not responsible ... I've spoilt you long enough ... all your life you have been spoilt ... men like you use repentance as a blind, so don't repent' (Chapter 38, p. 300).

All this damning indictment is true, but Margaret would have continued to spoil him if only he had allowed Helen to stay at Howards End. He again refuses a personal appeal (as he had when he decided to refuse Ruth's dying request that Margaret should have Howards End). He is too stupidly unimaginative to know what is important to other people and too selfish to care.

He has some virtues, which Margaret describes as 'secondary virtues'. He is energetic, efficient, kind within the strict limits of his imagination. But these qualities are not presented in the novel with any force; the reader has to take them on trust because Margaret, whom we admire and respect, loves him.

Charles Wilcox

Charles is something of a caricature, an exaggerated version of his father. He is commonly seen in connection with motor-car, raising clouds of dust. He bullies everybody, particularly servants ('Why be polite to servants? They don't understand it') and his wife. He is perpetually enraged at somebody else's inefficiency or suspicious that the Schlegels are in a conspiracy to rob him of his rightful inheritance. Unfortnately, he lacks even his father's capacity for making money. His reaction to Helen's seduction is the stock one: he must thrash the seducer within an inch of his life. But he miscalculates the measurement and goes to prison for manslaughter. He has no sense of guilt. All moral questions to him are plain black-and-white, all questions are simple, requiring a straight 'yes' or 'no' in reply.

Ruth Wilcox

It is impossible to write a character-study of Ruth Wilcox since she is less a character than a presence. She dies in the first third of the novel, yet her spirit lingers on, presiding over Howards End.

She 'had only one passion in life – her house' (Chapter 10, p. 95). Her life is rooted in one dear, particular place. The house belongs to her and she was born there. When she is at Howards End she is seen with a wisp of hay in her hand, 'trailing noiselessly across the lawn'. When she comes to London she is uprooted – she finds nothing to get up for in London.

She has an instinctive, even psychic, understanding of people and situations. She *knows* when Paul and Helen fall in love and when they love no longer. She is quiet, understanding that 'periods of quiet . . . are essential to true growth' (Chapter 10, p. 89). She dislikes hurry and change and intellectual chatter and thinks it wiser to leave 'action and discussion to men'. Yet she is capable of sharpness: she is hurt when Margaret at first refuses her invitation to visit Howards End.

Forster says that 'she was not intellectual, not even alert, and it was odd that, all the same, she should give the idea of greatness' (Chapter 9, p. 86). At another moment he calls her 'a woman of undefinable rarity'. This is something that we have to take on trust and there is more than a suspicion that Forster is passing off the word for the deed: the greatness is not presented and perhaps it cannot be. She lives by an 'inward light'. But Forster does manage to make her a continuing presence. She leaves Howards End to Margaret, and Margaret learns from her. Some of the spirit of Mrs Wilcox presides over the end of the book, particularly over the beautiful scene in which Margaret and Helen are reconciled.

Leonard Bast

Leonard is a poor young clerk who lives on the very edge of destitution. He *has* to worry about money because he has so little of it. He cannot afford to trust people – that is the privilege of the well-off. He has to worry about his lost umbrella and whether he can afford the price of a concert programme.

He tries to escape from the dreariness of his life through the pursuit of 'culture'. He goes to concerts, art galleries, opera, reads Ruskin (a Victorian critic of art and society, 1819–1900). But Leonard's culture is only a veneer; he is terrified that he will mispronounce foreign names, and what has Ruskin, the rich man in his gondola, to do with the realities of his life? He cannot get much beyond 'familiarity with the outside of books'. Leonard's 'case' convinces Margaret of the importance of money: 'independent thoughts are in nine cases out of ten the result of independent means'. And Forster says, 'He was inferior to most rich people ... he was not as courteous as the average rich man, nor as intelligent, nor as healthy, nor as lovable' (Chapter 6, p. 58).

Forster shows us Leonard's miserable home life in his basement flat and stacks the cards against him by saddling him with an ageing prostitute whom he has 'honourably' promised to marry. One night he goes for a walk to see the dawn, in imitation of the authors he has been reading. He tells the Schlegel sisters, who are particularly impressed by the honesty with which he answers, 'with unforgettable sincerity', 'No', to Helen's question whether the dawn was wonderful.

The Schlegels invite him to tea in order to tell him about the imminent crash of the Porphyrion Insurance Company, but Leonard wants to talk about books, and feels that he is being pumped and patronized. He goes to the Schlegels in order to escape from the Porphyrion, not be be reminded of it. Nevertheless, he accepts the advice and is ruined. From now on, Leonard is an unwilling victim, particularly of Helen, who takes him up as a 'cause'. He is dragged against his will to Shropshire, 'enticed' by Helen, and eventually falls to the degradation of sponging on his relations. He feels a useless remorse and keeps our sympathy by his tenderness towards Jacky. He is killed by a combination of the Wilcox self-righteousness and the Schlegel culture.

His child will inherit Howards End. It is not easy to be sure what Forster intended by this. Leonard is essentially a good man who has been stunted by the inhuman world in which he has had to live. He is a wage-slave, a cog in the machine which the Wilcoxes have built and which eventually destroys him. Will the baby have the chance to grow into the man that Leonard had no chance to be? Or is Forster prophesying the breakdown of the class system of the Edwardian world, and the reign of the proletariat? At any rate the ending of the book seems to suggest hope – just.

Dolly

'Dolly looked silly, and had one of those triangular faces that so often prove attractive to a robust man' (Chapter 8, p. 81). There is little to her: she is almost as vacuous a character as Jacky, to whom she is implicitly linked by the fact that they both have their photographs broken. She is bullied by Charles and takes refuge in her children. She is an excellent machine for the reproduction of Wilcoxes. She likes gossip and provides Margaret with useful information. It is she who, at the end of the book, tactlessly reveals the fact that, at her death, Ruth Wilcox had left Howards End to Margaret – a nice comic touch.

Aunt Juley

She is essentially kindly and well-intentioned, but interfering and inquisitive: she spends much of her time at Wickham Place watching the flats opposite. Promising to be tactful, she goes to Howards End to 'make inquiries' about Helen's affair with Paul and makes a comic muddle of the expedition. She is a pillar of the cultural life of Swanage and deeply suspicious of foreigners.

Jacky

An ageing prostitute who is slipping down into the 'colourless years'. She seems an idle, amiable slut. The scene in which she confronts her ex-lover, Henry, is one of the least convincing in the book. Forster clearly knew little about her kind and isn't concerned to invent much.

Evie

A healthy, tennis-playing Wilcox, good-hearted enough. Charles blames her for her father's marriage to Margaret, since, if she had not stopped looking after him in order to marry, he would not have been so lonely.

Paul

At the beginning of the story, Paul is at hand for Helen to 'fall in love with'. Helen is, in fact, in love with the whole family, but she focuses her emotions briefly and powerfully on Paul. He is in the mood to flirt with 'any pretty girl', and something inside him whispers, 'This girl would let you kiss her' – so he takes his chance.

Next day, the affair comes to a brisk end: Paul looks frightened, afraid that he may have committed himself further than – with the hindsight of his practical daylight mind – he had intended. Nevertheless, the brief experience of falling in love makes a deep and lasting impression on Helen.

Paul reappears at the end of the book. His time abroad has made him into the worst kind of Wilcox: ill-tempered, ungracious and suspicious.

Miss Avery

Miss Avery is a mysterious, 'odd' figure. Margaret respects her, but the other Wilcoxes think she is mad. She represents the continuity of Howards End (almost as the 'familiar spirit' of the place). She has been devoted to Ruth, the first Mrs Wilcox, and recognizes in Margaret her true heir: at their first encounter Miss Avery appears to mistake Margaret for Ruth.

When Miss Avery sends Evie Wilcox a pendant, as a wedding present in memory of Evie's mother, Evie sends it back — the Wilcoxes having interpreted the expensive present as a device for securing a wedding invitation. Miss Avery, indignant, writes a rude letter to Evie, and throws the pendant into the duckpond!

She seems, like Mrs Wilcox herself, to have the power of seeing into the future. She believes, rightly, that Margaret will one day live at Howards End: she arranges all Margaret's furniture (which had simply been sent to the house for temporary storage) throughout the rooms of the house. Miss Avery has the insight that is perhaps a development of human sympathy. It is she who remarks tenderly about Leonard Bast, 'No one ever told the lad he'll have a child.'

Style

Though the overall design of the book seems in some ways unsatisfactory, it is consistently interesting because Forster is a master of English prose and he uses his command of prose to remind us of, and give new insight into, values that are always in danger and need to be defended.

Forster's style is very flexible. He is a master also of social comedy — as in the scene between Mrs Munt and Charles at the beginning, or Margaret's 'business' conversation with Henry after their engagement. He can reveal worlds of character in an apparently trivial incident, as when the car runs over the 'rotton cat'. He is master of the astonishingly apt image: Henry's furniture looks 'as if a motor-car had spawned' — the word 'spawned' suggesting the copulation of toads. His description of Margaret's reactions during the car journey evoke remarkably well the sensation of disorientation — and disorientation in the face of the developing commercial world is one of the themes of the novel. He can shift his tone cleverly from moment to moment, with subtly modulating shades of irony: so, after Helen has been trying unsuccessfully but frantically to ensure that Leonard gets her five thousand pounds, he says: 'Then she reinvested, and, owing to the good advice of her stockbrokers, became rather richer than she had been before.' He can manage a sentence of simple farce, of the kind Wodehouse would have been proud of: 'Evie heard of her father's engagement when she was in for a tennis tournament and her play went simply to pot' — and we need to know nothing more about Evie.

Forster is fond of interpolating little remarks or incidents whose meaning we can only understand at a later stage: Margaret points out in a long letter to Helen the need for charity in sexual matters, and Helen merely thanks her for her kind letter; later, we realize that Helen is pregnant. Mrs

Wilcox reveals that Henry has built a garage in what used to be the paddock for the pony; only later do we hear that the paddock was particularly dear to Mrs Wilcox, a fact Henry was too blind to realize.

The author himself is nearly always present, directing the reader's response. He will stand aside from his narrative to debate whether Henry and Charles were right not to obey Mrs Wilcox's dying wish to leave Howards End to Margaret, or to meditate amusingly on weddings. This authorial presence may be contrary to modern taste, but in Forster's case we may well be glad to be in contact with such a witty, delicate and subtle mind. Sometimes, however, his tact deserts him. He can overwrite, as in some of the patriotic passages: 'England was alive, throbbing through all her estuaries, crying for joy through the mouths of all her gulls, and the north wind, with contrary motion, blew stronger against her rising seas.' He seems here to have been carried away too easily on the wings of rhythm. And the element of 'poetic' mysticism seems sadly misjudged: 'I feel that you and I and Henry are only fragments of that woman's mind. She knows everything. She is the house, and the tree that leans over it' etc.

Forster orchestrates his novel by the use of the recurrent phrase, or 'leitmotif': 'panic and emptiness'; 'telegrams and anger'; 'see life steadily and see it whole'; 'the inner life'. They are part of the rhythm of the novel, on which Forster set high value (see the chapter 'Pattern and Rhythm' in *Aspects of the Novel*) and which he defined as 'repetition plus variation'. The novel is also full of natural things used symbolically or at least with a significance that reaches beyond the actual objects: the wisp of hay; the wych-elm; motor-cars; the Schlegel sword; and Howards End itself. It is always wrong to try to pin such things down too precisely; if they're successful they will work of their own accord.

Finally, an example of Forster's controlled, balanced, evaluating prose at its best; the Wilcoxes are leaving Oniton for the last time: 'It is not their names which recur in the parish register. It is not their ghosts that sigh among the alders at evening. They have swept into the valley and swept out of it, leaving a little dust and a little money behind' (Chapter 29, p. 246).

General questions and sample answer in note form

1 Illustrate Forster's use of humour in the novel.
2 What has Forster to say about the condition of England at the time he was writing?
3 What are the particular qualities of the Wilcox mind?
4 Discuss the role of Howards End in the novel.
5 Forster said that the theme of the novel was 'the hunt for a home'. Illustrate this.
6 What is the importance of Mrs Wilcox?
7 What are the main differences between Margaret and Helen?
8 D. H. Lawrence praised the portrait of Leonard Bast. Do you think it is a good portrait?
9 What part does the motor-car play in the novel?
10 Write about Tibby's contribution to the novel.
11 'Only connect'. Is this a satisfactory epigraph for the book?
12 Do you think that Henry Wilcox is too stupid for Forster's purposes?
13 How would you answer the charge that Margaret's marriage with Henry is improbable?
14 Why does Helen have her 'affair' with Leonard?
15 In what sense is *Howards End* a feminist novel?
16 What is the importance of money in the novel?
17 Discuss the extent of Forster's use of coincidence in the book.
18 What do you think are the main weaknesses of the book?
19 Discuss Forster's use of symbols.
20 Discuss in detail the scene which seems to you to be the most moving in the book.
21 On the evidence of *Howards End*, what values does Forster consider to be supreme?

22 How satisfactory do you find the ending of the book?

23 Do you find Forster's presence in the book too obtrusive?

24 What are the main characters of Forster's style?

Suggested notes for essay answer to question 1

(a) *Introduction* – *very brief* plot summary in order to indicate the nature of the novel – then introduce types of humour – author's use of own voice – conception and presentation of character – leading to

(b) *Irony* – the Forsterian modes – authorial – character (instance Mr Wilcox, Charles, Helen, Tibby) and the black humour involving Charles, for example, the nature of the humour in the presentation of Miss Avery.

(c) Contemplation of society – class differences – presentation of Leonard Bast and Jacky – humour of incident – emphases on the power of the motor-car; irony here and with regard to money and property, etc.

(d) Forster's tone – whimsical – indulgent – mocking – occasionally satirical (quote in support of these and any other aspects of tone which you feel relevant).

(e) Conclusion – range of comedy – humour through dialogue with the balancing humour of description – attitude – perspective – humour in brief turns of phrase, part of mature comic control.

Further reading

Other novels by E. M. Forster, and particularly:
A Room with a View
Where Angels Fear to Tread
A Passage to India
E. M. Forster, A Critical Study, Laurence Brander (Hart-Davis, MacGibbon)
E. M. Forster, The Personal Voice, John Colmer (Routledge & Kegan Paul)
The Writings of E M. Forster, Rose Macaulay (Hogarth Press)
E. M. Forster, Lionel Trilling (Hogarth Press)
E. M. Forster: A Life, P. N. Furbank (Oxford University Press)

Brodie's Notes

D. H. Lawrence	The Rainbow
D. H. Lawrence	Sons and Lovers
D. H. Lawrence	Women in Love
Harper Lee	To Kill a Mockingbird
Laurie Lee	Cider with Rosie
Christopher Marlowe	Dr Faustus
Arthur Miller	The Crucible
Arthur Miller	Death of a Salesman
John Milton	Paradise Lost
Robert C. O'Brien	Z for Zachariah
Sean O'Casey	Juno and the Paycock
George Orwell	Animal Farm
George Orwell	1984
J. B. Priestley	An Inspector Calls
J. D. Salinger	The Catcher in the Rye
William Shakespeare	Antony and Cleopatra
William Shakespeare	As You Like It
William Shakespeare	Hamlet
William Shakespeare	Henry IV Part I
William Shakespeare	Julius Caesar
William Shakespeare	King Lear
William Shakespeare	Macbeth
William Shakespeare	Measure for Measure
William Shakespeare	The Merchant of Venice
William Shakespeare	A Midsummer Night's Dream
William Shakespeare	Much Ado about Nothing
William Shakespeare	Othello
William Shakespeare	Richard II
William Shakespeare	Romeo and Juliet
William Shakespeare	The Tempest
William Shakespeare	Twelfth Night
George Bernard Shaw	Pygmalion
Alan Sillitoe	Selected Fiction
John Steinbeck	Of Mice and Men and The Pearl
Jonathan Swift	Gulliver's Travels
Dylan Thomas	Under Milk Wood
Alice Walker	The Color Purple
W. B. Yeats	Selected Poetry

ENGLISH COURSEWORK BOOKS

Terri Apter	Women and Society
Kevin Dowling	Drama and Poetry
Philip Gooden	Conflict
Philip Gooden	Science Fiction
Margaret K. Gray	Modern Drama
Graham Handley	Modern Poetry
Graham Handley	Prose
Graham Handley	Childhood and Adolescence
R. J. Sims	The Short Story